ASIA SMALL AND MEDIUM-SIZED ENTERPRISE MONITOR 2024

VOLUME II: TRENDS AND CHALLENGES FACING SMALL BUSINESSES IN TIMOR-LESTE—KEY SURVEY FINDINGS

FEBRUARY 2025

ASIAN DEVELOPMENT BANK

CONTENTS

Tables and Figures   iv

Foreword   v

Acknowledgments   vi

Abbreviations   vii

Executive Summary   viii

1. Introduction   1

2. Macroeconomic Conditions   2

3. Methodology and Data   3

4. Micro, Small, and Medium-Sized Enterprise Profile   4

5. Survey Findings   12
    A. Business Environment   12
    B. Revenue   13
    C. Employment and Wages   13
    D. Logistics   15
    E. Financial Conditions and Funding   15
    F. What Small Businesses Want from Government   18

6. Policy Implications   21

7. Conclusion   23

Appendix: Survey Questionnaire   25

TABLES AND FIGURES

Tables

1	Sampling Frame and Data Collected	3
2	Part-Time or Contractual Workers	7

Figures

1	Timor-Leste Economy	2
2	Profile of Firms Surveyed	4
3	Sector and Regional Distribution	5
4	Company Age, Ownership, and Employees	6
5	Assets, Sales Income, and Wages	8
6	Business Digitalization	9
7	Micro, Small, and Medium-Sized Enterprise Trade	10
8	Share of Export and Import Business and Destination	11
9	Business Environment	12
10	Firm Revenue (July 2023–July 2024)	13
11	Employment and Wages	14
12	Logistics	15
13	Financial Condition	16
14	Funding	17
15	Funding Demand, Source, and Constraints	18
16	Nonfinancial Policy Measures Desired	19
17	Financial Policy Measures Desired	20

FOREWORD

Historically, Timor-Leste has had low economic growth due to both external and domestic shocks. The medium-to-long-term policy challenge is to transform the economy into one driven by a strong private sector that promotes robust and sustainable growth. Despite occasional disruptions, post-pandemic growth momentum has continued in Timor-Leste. While gross domestic product growth slowed from 4.0% in 2022 to 2.4% in 2023, output is forecast to expand by 3.1% in 2024 and 3.9% in 2025, driven mainly by increased private consumption, investment, foreign tourism, and remittances. Inflation is expected to remain low at 2.9% in 2025. Strengthening the conditions to support micro, small, and medium-sized enterprise (MSME) growth is crucial for supporting resilient growth and diversifying beyond a natural resource-oriented growth model.

In July 2024, the Asian Development Bank (ADB), in collaboration with the Timor-Leste Ministry of Commerce and Industry, conducted a business mapping survey to help the government design an evidenced-based, workable national MSME development policy. The survey was jointly financed by ADB's two technical assistance projects, "Upgrading the Asia Small and Medium-Sized Enterprise Monitor" and "Capacity for Multilateral and Regional Economic Integration." The survey was the first-ever large-scale business mapping exercise, and its success was largely due to collaborative efforts of ADB's Economic Research and Development Impact Department and Timor-Leste Resident Mission of the Southeast Asia Department, and government counterparts. This report contributes to Timor-Leste's efforts to join the Association of Southeast Asian Nations. It should help the government to develop effective policies to support future MSME development.

Albert Park
Chief Economist and Director General
Economic Research and Development Impact Department
Asian Development Bank

ACKNOWLEDGMENTS

The Asia Small and Medium-Sized Enterprise Monitor 2024 Volume II was prepared by several economists: Shigehiro Shinozaki as lead author and senior economist at the Economic Research and Development Impact Department (ERDI) of the Asian Development Bank (ADB); Stefania Dina, country director of the Timor-Leste Resident Mission (TLRM) of the Southeast Asia Department (SERD); Bold Sandagdorj, TLRM country economist, and Kavita Iyengar, senior country economist of SERD's Lao People's Democratic Republic Resident Mission. The business mapping survey was helped by the Ministry of Commerce and Industry, Investment and Export Promotion Agency, the Chamber of Commerce and Industry of Timor-Leste, the National Institute of Statistics of Timor-Leste, and the Faculty of Economics and Management of the National University of Timor-Leste. The survey was jointly financed, specifically under ERDI's TA 9746-REG: "Upgrading the Asia Small and Medium-Sized Enterprise Monitor" and TA 6542-TIM: "Capacity for Multilateral and Regional Economic Integration" under SERD. An Indonesia-based research firm—Yayasan Akademika—conducted the field survey covering all 13 municipalities of Timor-Leste, guided by Shigehiro Shinozaki. It was supported by Jong Woo Kang, director of the Regional Cooperation and Integration Division, and James Villafuerte, ERDI regional lead economist. Paulo Rodelio Halili and Angel Love Roque provided administrative support. Guy Sacerdoti copyedited the report, Maria Guia de Guzman proofread it, and Jess Alfonso Macasaet did page proof checking. The report was reviewed by the Government of Timor-Leste.

ABBREVIATIONS

ADB	–	Asian Development Bank
ASEAN	–	Association of Southeast Asian Nations
BDS	–	business development services
COVID-19	–	coronavirus disease
ICT	–	information and communication technology
MSME	–	micro, small, and medium-sized enterprise

EXECUTIVE SUMMARY

The Asian Development Bank (ADB), in collaboration with the Timor-Leste Ministry of Commerce and Industry, conducted a business mapping survey to assist the government in designing a workable, evidence-based report (MSME) development policy. The survey results are a crucial component of ADB's broader support for Timor-Leste's accession to the Association of Southeast Asian Nations (ASEAN).

The business mapping survey described MSME business conditions and performance as of July 2024. MSMEs in Timor-Leste are mostly self-employed or microenterprises with small monthly revenues, typically stability-oriented firms in distributive trade with limited markets. Tourism-related MSMEs are a small fraction of the country's MSMEs. Male workers dominate MSME employees. Worker benefits are limited or nonexistent. MSMEs operate using part-time or contractual workers. Growth-oriented firms and innovative entrepreneurship have yet to develop. Following the coronavirus disease (COVID-19) pandemic, a small fraction of MSMEs joined the e-commerce market. There are few MSMEs in international trade, with most mainly importing goods/raw materials from Indonesia. There is growth potential in young firms, start-ups, and women-led MSMEs, which account for about half the MSMEs surveyed. Designing, developing, and implementing an MSME strategy that focuses on promoting green MSMEs will be central in diversifying the economy.

The MSME business environment remains relatively stable, with most businesses feeling either optimistic or unworried over future prospects. However, a relatively large share of women-led MSMEs feel that higher production costs will lead to worse business conditions. Two-thirds of MSMEs reported that sales revenues rose or remained steady, with the remaining third reporting annual revenue losses, particularly among women-led MSMEs. Both employment and wage conditions were stable among MSMEs, less affected by external shocks. A small fraction of MSMEs faced supply chain bottlenecks.

More than two-thirds of MSMEs felt that they were financially stable—with sufficient savings and assets to maintain business for over 6 months—while about 30% had no savings or would run out of funds in 6 months. Most MSMEs felt that their small size allowed them to manage their business using their own funds. Bank credit supplements working capital when required, more so among women-led MSMEs. There are few short-term funding needs among MSMEs. Many require small amounts of working capital (up to $20,000) for 6 months operations. However, many MSMEs worry over future business prospects due to declining purchasing power, limited market growth, and rising costs for production and logistics—all suggesting a need for more funding in the future.

MSMEs look to the government for assistance through business subsidies, tax relief, business development services (BDS), easier access to public procurement, and worker skill development. Surprisingly, there was relatively little demand for government support in business digitalization and international trade (such as a one-stop service window). Respondents cited the need for various forms of financial assistance, including business restructuring funds, simplified loan procedures, trade finance and supply chain finance, along with concessional lending schemes. Demand for concessional lending and credit guarantees was relatively higher for women-led MSMEs than those led by men. The low demand for digital financial services can be explained in part by low levels of financial literacy, little awareness of available products, limited internet connectivity, and a lack of trust due to worries over security and fraud.

The government has implemented several measures to address private sector constraints and construct a legal and regulatory framework that promotes competitiveness, particularly among MSMEs. The business mapping survey showed, however, that challenges remain. As next steps, seven policy implications were particularly highlighted to boost MSME development:

1. Strengthening the **focused approach** toward MSME support—promoting a growth and graduation cycle of enterprises and encouraging green MSMEs. Beyond traditional distributive trade, technology-based MSMEs—including those employing green technology and digitalization—should be prioritized with assistance focused on increasing business literacy and development programs.
2. Developing national **business clustering** to create a base of young and innovative entrepreneurs—making the best use of firms led by the youth, women, those using green technologies, and those promoting tourism. Linking the development of agricultural value chains (such as coffee and organic oils) with ecotourism (for example, coffee plantation agritourism) is one promising area for development.
3. Making the **export business** more attractive for MSMEs—and joining global value chains—can be helped by strengthening national product branding, BDS, upgrading skills, as well as developing hard infrastructure. Increased regional tensions in the Middle East and elsewhere accelerated supply chain disruptions globally, resulting in surging trade costs. Thus, strengthening supply chain networks and improving hard infrastructure is critical for MSME exporters to become competitive.
4. Promoting **business digitalization** for MSMEs to expand their businesses will ultimately lower costs. Business digitalization remains low among MSMEs in Timor-Leste, with many uninterested largely due to a lack of digital literacy. Thus, enhancing digital literacy should be prioritized with improved information and communication technology infrastructure.
5. There remains a huge potential among female workers for eventual **job creation**, particularly through skill upgrading. This should be aligned with plans to create a base of growth-oriented firms and innovative entrepreneurship.
6. Strengthening **financial literacy** among MSMEs and developing **alternative financing options** for qualified businesses can improve access to growth capital. Developing digital finance solutions should also be a priority.
7. Preparing **a comprehensive mid- to long-term national MSME development strategy** with accompanying monitor framework is essential. Creating regular periodically updated MSME landscape data is what backs evidence-based, feasible policy interventions for MSME development.

The results of the survey showed large similarities between MSMEs in Timor-Leste. Most are self-employed, trading their preferred goods and services among a small, mostly known market. There are few vibrant, innovative, growth-oriented firms. These can be helped first by removing the infrastructure bottlenecks—such as ICT and transportation—that currently inhibit or block the development of firms with new ideas—innovators, start-ups, and those with entrepreneurial instinct. Beyond this basic foundation, there are three important elements that can help build a strong base of growth-oriented firms in Timor-Leste:

1. The **mindset** of MSME owners and managers should shift from the more passive stability-oriented outlook to a more growth-oriented strategy;
2. **MSMEs need skilled workers technologically capable of expanding business both domestically and globally; and**
3. MSMEs must become **formalized** businesses to make use of the growth opportunities available. This can be supported by strengthening business literacy programs for MSMEs, BDS, and skill upgrade training for MSME workers (especially in gender-focused training).

With a population of just 1.3 million people, internationalizing MSMEs will definitely diversify the economy. But as global geopolitical conflicts disrupt supply chains both regionally and globally, the resulting higher trade costs raise the barrier to boosting MSME exports. Business clustering is one promising solution for managing MSME production costs, strengthening market networks, and increasing the competitiveness of MSME exports.

Business digitalization is rare among MSMEs in Timor-Leste, particularly limited among the majority stability-oriented firms. Promoting business digitalization among MSMEs is a key component of the government's MSME policy design. The government will need to create incentive schemes to attract growth-oriented small firms and innovative entrepreneurs. For example, there are various support programs in other developing Asian economies—such as tax incentives, grants for adopting technology and commercialization, subsidies for e-commerce, and legal reforms. Developing a centralized policy framework to implement MSME digitalization should be well designed nationally.

The survey found that male workers dominate the MSME workforce. Women and youth remain underserved resources for building resilient, sustainable growth across developing Asia. As in other countries, a gender-responsive growth model should be a major part of any national MSME development strategy. Almost half (46.5%) of women-led MSMEs are young start-ups operating for 5 years or less. To encourage more women and younger aged workers, more gender-focused skills training, business literacy programs, and BDS should be strengthened. Also important is to map out factors affecting women and young entrepreneurship development nationally.

According to the survey findings, tourism-related MSMEs were just a small fraction of the country total. As an idea to promote the tourism industry by using MSME resources, ecotourism addressing coffee plantations and other agriproducts and through marine sports will suit to Timor-Leste.

Promoting green MSMEs is a critical policy priority. Green MSMEs—defined as socially responsive firms adopting environmental, social, and governance principles and using green technologies—should be supported by appropriate government financial and nonfinancial measures. Business consulting and marketing services, financial schemes such as climate bonds to help finance MSMEs, and government assistance like subsidies and tax incentives can help build a national base of green MSMEs.

Timor-Leste is the youngest country in Asia, gaining independence in May 2002. It aims for ASEAN accession this year. Establishing a comprehensive national MSME policy with time-bound workable action plans would be a critical concrete step in realizing its ASEAN accession goal.

1. INTRODUCTION

Timor-Leste is a small island country with a population of 1.3 million. It is the youngest country in Asia, gaining independence in May 2002. In 2023, the poverty rate remained high at 41.8%, based on the national poverty rate, and 48.3% according to the Global Multidimensional Poverty Index.[1] Given the country's heavy reliance on the petroleum sector, it is critically important to diversify the economy into areas that can support more resilient, sustainable growth. Here, private sector development becomes a central priority, with micro, small, and medium-sized enterprises (MSMEs) expected to play a pivotal role in economic diversification.

With this in mind, the government enacted a law on MSME support measures in 2023 (Decree No.30 of 2023). The assistance measures focus mainly on business incubation—to provide essential training, seed funding, concessional financing, and credit guarantees. The law classifies firm's size by (i) the number of employees, and (ii) annual sales revenue/turnover or annual total assets excluding land (Article 4). A microenterprise is defined as a firm with up to five employees and annual turnover not exceeding $5,000 or annual total assets of not more than $25,000. A small enterprise has 6–20 employees, an annual turnover not exceeding $50,000 or annual total assets of not more than $150,000. A medium-sized firm employs 21–50 workers with an annual turnover not exceeding $1 million or annual total assets of not exceeding $250,000.

As of the end of 2024, a comprehensive policy action plan for MSME development had not yet been prepared, primarily due to a lack of data. To address this gap in landscape data, the Asian Development Bank (ADB) conducted a business mapping survey throughout Timor-Leste in July 2024 in cooperation with the Ministry of Commerce and Industry. The main objective of the survey is to better understand the business environment and assist the government in designing an evidence-based national MSME development policy. The survey is part of ADB's support for the Government of Timor-Leste in its accession to the Association of Southeast Asian Nations (ASEAN). This report lays out the key survey findings and discusses primary policy implications.

---

[1]   UNDP and Oxford Poverty and Human Development Initiative (OPHI). 2023. Global Multidimensional Poverty Index 2023.

2. MACROECONOMIC CONDITIONS

Despite some disruptions, economic growth momentum in Timor-Leste continues, with inflation remaining moderate. Growth in gross domestic product slowed to 2.4% in 2023 but is forecast to expand by 3.1% in 2024 and 3.9% in 2025 (Figure 1A). Inflation is forecast to increase slightly from 2.1% in 2024 to 2.9% in 2025, though it remains relatively low (Figure 1B). Increased private consumption, investments, foreign tourist receipts, and remittances contribute to robust growth. MSMEs underpin this resilient growth despite challenges such as global geopolitical tensions and climate change. Strengthening MSME dynamics will help diversify the economy beyond its oil and natural gas roots.

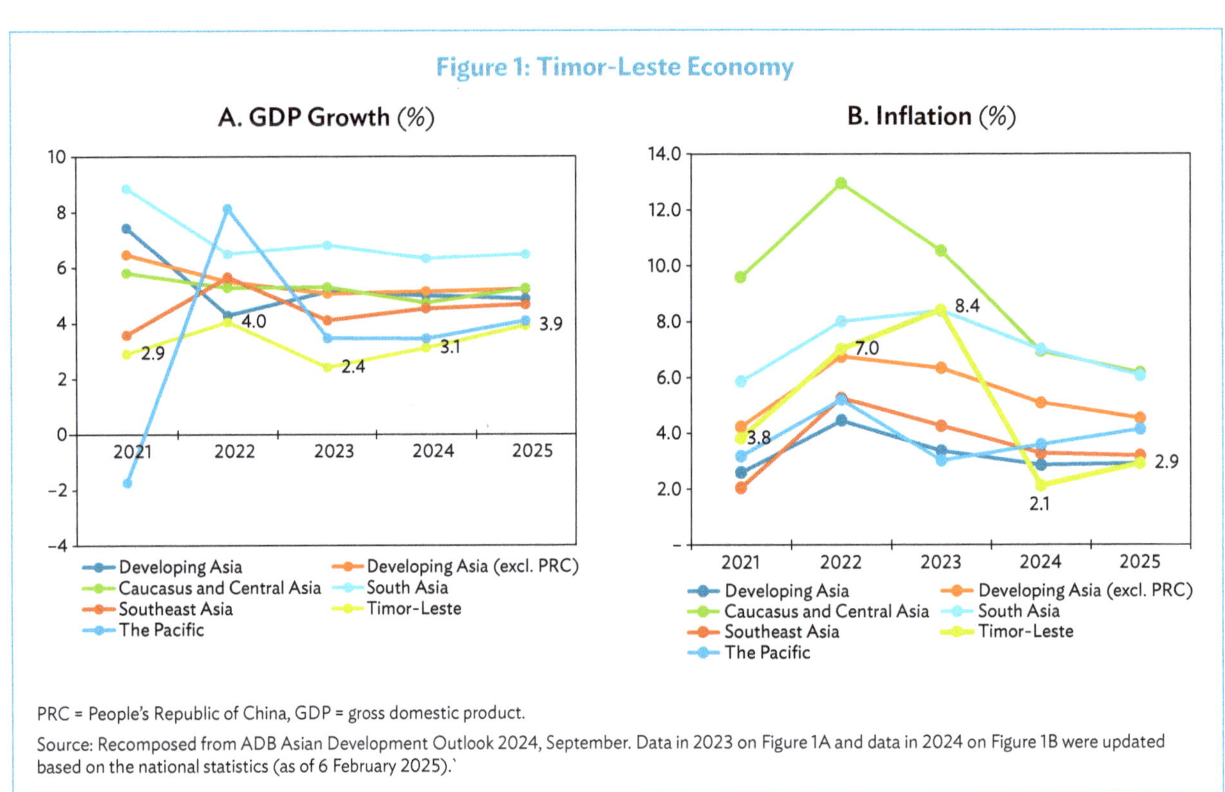

PRC = People's Republic of China, GDP = gross domestic product.

Source: Recomposed from ADB Asian Development Outlook 2024, September. Data in 2023 on Figure 1A and data in 2024 on Figure 1B were updated based on the national statistics (as of 6 February 2025).`

3. METHODOLOGY AND DATA

The field survey was conducted across all 13 Timor-Leste municipalities during 5–21 July 2024, using a standardized business survey questionnaire comprising three components: (i) company profile, (ii) business environment, and (iii) policy interventions (Appendix). The questionnaire was translated into the local language, Tetum. Thirty qualified enumerators were hired through a local consulting firm (the Indonesia-based research firm Yayasan Akademika) in cooperation with the Faculty of Economics and Management of the National University of Timor-Leste. After training, they conducted direct interviews with target MSME respondents in designated municipalities (Groups I–III). ADB monitored and controlled the field survey in close to real time.

Due to the limited data available—and that the majority of MSMEs are self-employed—a quasi-sampling frame was developed based on labor force population aged 10 years old and over by municipality, using the Timor-Leste Population and Housing Census 2022 (Table 1). Following the sampling frame, respondents were randomly selected based on the business directory received from the Investment and Export Promotion Agency (*TradeInvest*) and Ministry of Commerce and Industry. MSME survey classifications referred to the employment threshold under Decree No.30 of 2023: (i) a firm with up to five employees as microenterprise, (ii) a firm with 6–20 employees as a small enterprise, and (iii) a firm with 21–50 employees as a medium-sized enterprise. A total of 3,080 valid samples from 13 municipalities were collected.

Table 1: Sampling Frame and Data Collected

Municipality	City	Total population, 2022	Aged 10 years old and over (labor force population)	% share	Target samples	Data collected	% share
Group I					**1,177**	**1,189**	
Dili	Dili	324,738	252,373	24.7%	741	767	24.9%
Atauro (part of Dili)		10,295	8,051	0.8%	24		
Aileu	Aileu	54,324	40,469	4.0%	119	124	4.0%
Ainaro	Ainaro	73,115	54,152	5.3%	159	159	5.2%
Manufahi	Sama	60,665	46,186	4.5%	136	139	4.5%
Group II					**751**	**787**	
Baucau	Baucau	134,878	102,684	10.0%	301	307	10.0%
Manatuto	Manatuto	50,859	38,820	3.8%	114	127	4.1%
Viqueque	Viqueque	80,176	61,464	6.0%	180	190	6.2%
Lautem	Lospalos	70,022	52,969	5.2%	155	163	5.3%
Group III					**1,071**	**1,104**	
Ermera	Gleno	137,750	103,470	10.1%	304	310	10.1%
Liquica	Liquica	83,658	62,504	6.1%	183	191	6.2%
Bobonaro	Maliana	106,639	80,835	7.9%	237	242	7.9%
Cova Lima	Suai	73,933	56,112	5.5%	165	173	5.6%
Oecusse	Pante Macassar	80,685	62,173	6.1%	182	188	6.1%
	Total	**1,341,737**	**1,022,262**	**100%**	**3,000**	**3,080**	**100%**

Source: Calculated based on the Timor-Leste Population and Housing Census 2022. Sector distribution and firm size distribution are unavailable.

4. MICRO, SMALL, AND MEDIUM-SIZED ENTERPRISE PROFILE

- 50.4% of the respondents were self-employed, 42.6% from microenterprises, with 6.6% from small firms, and 0.5% medium-sized.
- 71.6% were registered firms, 13.0% were unregistered (informal) firms, 14.7% were individual entrepreneurs, and 0.6% were cooperatives or foundations.
- 44.4% worked in trade, with 21.7% in accommodation/food services, 12.0% in manufacturing, 11.3% in other services, and 2.5% in agriculture.
- 47.4% were young start-ups operating for 5 years or less.
- 43.2% firms were women-led.
- 8.0% were digitally operated firms using e-commerce.
- 10.2% worked in the export/import business.

In Timor-Leste, MSMEs are mostly self-employed or microenterprises. Half (50.4%) of the respondents were self-employed, with 42.6% from microenterprises, 6.6% from small firms, with just 0.5% from medium-sized firms (Figure 2A). By type, 71.6% were registered firms, while 13% were unregistered (informal) with 14.7% individual entrepreneurs (Figure 2B). Tourism-related MSMEs are a small fraction of the country's MSMEs. Tourism is a cross-cutting industry involving accommodation, restaurants, retail trade (such as handicrafts and souvenir shops), transportation, and tourist agencies. This report classifies tourism-related firms as those that belong to tourism organizations or tourism associations, which accounted for just 2.8% of total respondents (Figure 2C).

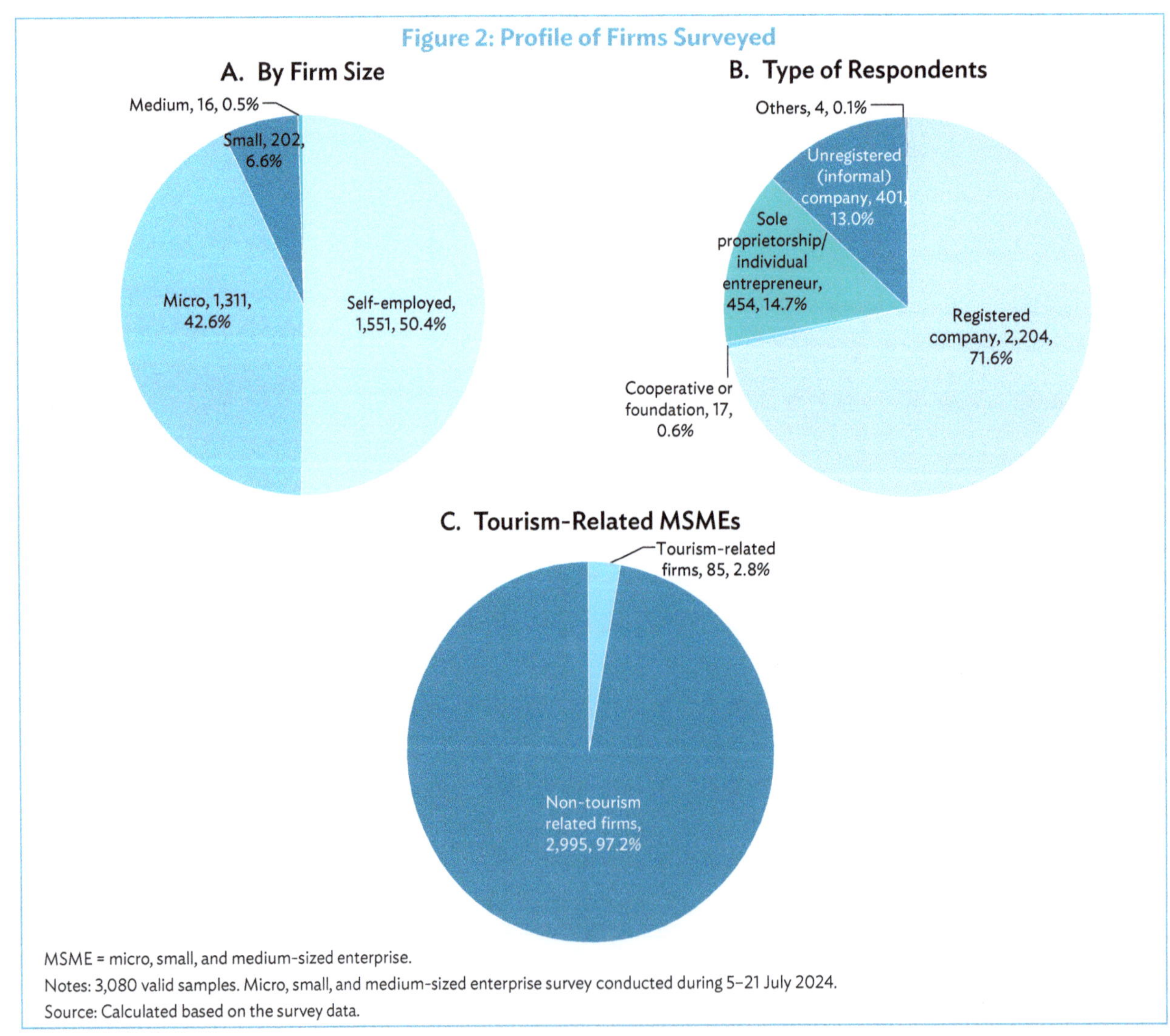

Figure 2: Profile of Firms Surveyed

MSME = micro, small, and medium-sized enterprise.
Notes: 3,080 valid samples. Micro, small, and medium-sized enterprise survey conducted during 5–21 July 2024.
Source: Calculated based on the survey data.

By sector, 44.4% were in wholesale and retail trade, with 21.7% in accommodation and food services, 12.0% in manufacturing, 11.3% in other services, and 2.5% in agriculture (Figure 3A). Most MSMEs worked in distributive trade, operating around central cities (Figure 3B).[2]

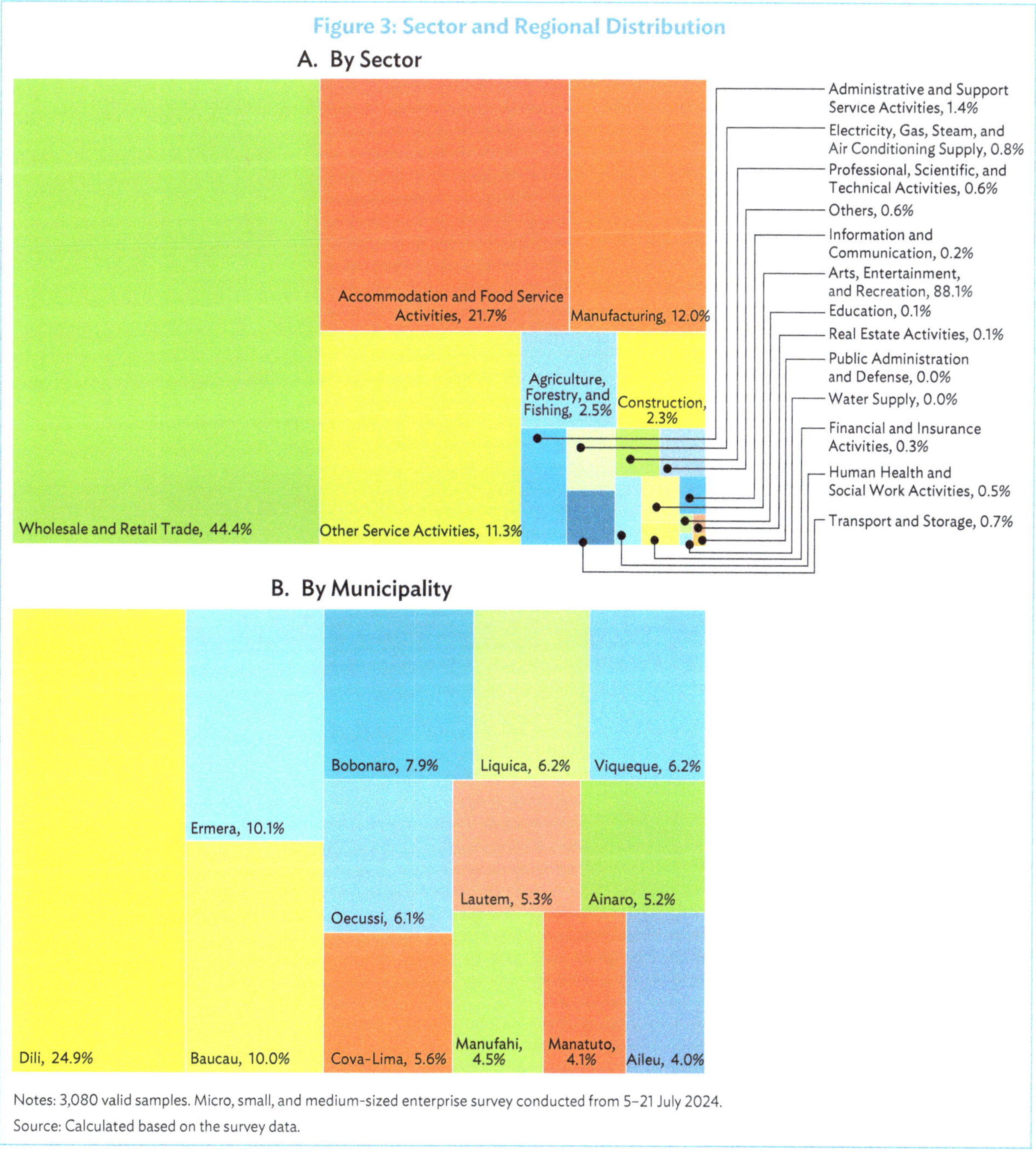

Notes: 3,080 valid samples. Micro, small, and medium-sized enterprise survey conducted from 5–21 July 2024.
Source: Calculated based on the survey data.

[2]   The respondents were sampled following the labor force structure by municipality; hence, the regional distribution of surveyed firms is consistent with the labor force distribution in 2022.

Most firms operating in Timor-Leste are relatively young. Nearly half (47.4%) were young start-ups—operating for up to 5 years—with 27.7% in business for 6–10 years. Some 13.8% had 11-15 years of operations, 10.0% had 16–30 years operations, with just 1.1% with over 31 years experience (Figure 4A). In essence, over 90% of MSMEs began operations after independence in 2002.

Interestingly, nearly half (43.2%) of the firms surveyed were women-led with the rest (56.8%) led by men (Figure 4B). Yet, male workers clearly dominate the MSME workforce. The majority of MSMEs (83.6%) reported that female workers accounted for 10% or less of employees (Figure 4C). Female workers accounted for 11%–30% of employees in 8.8% of the surveyed firms. Those with more than 50% female employees accounted for less than 4% of the firms surveyed. Clearly, there is room for improvement. Those self-employed and working for microenterprises filled labor shortages by hiring part-time or contractual workers (Table 2).

The MSME working environment could be improved in several ways. Employees benefits are quite limited among MSMEs, with just 9.8% of MSMEs surveyed offering a social security system for employees. Over 80% provide no assistance for employees at all (Figure 4D).

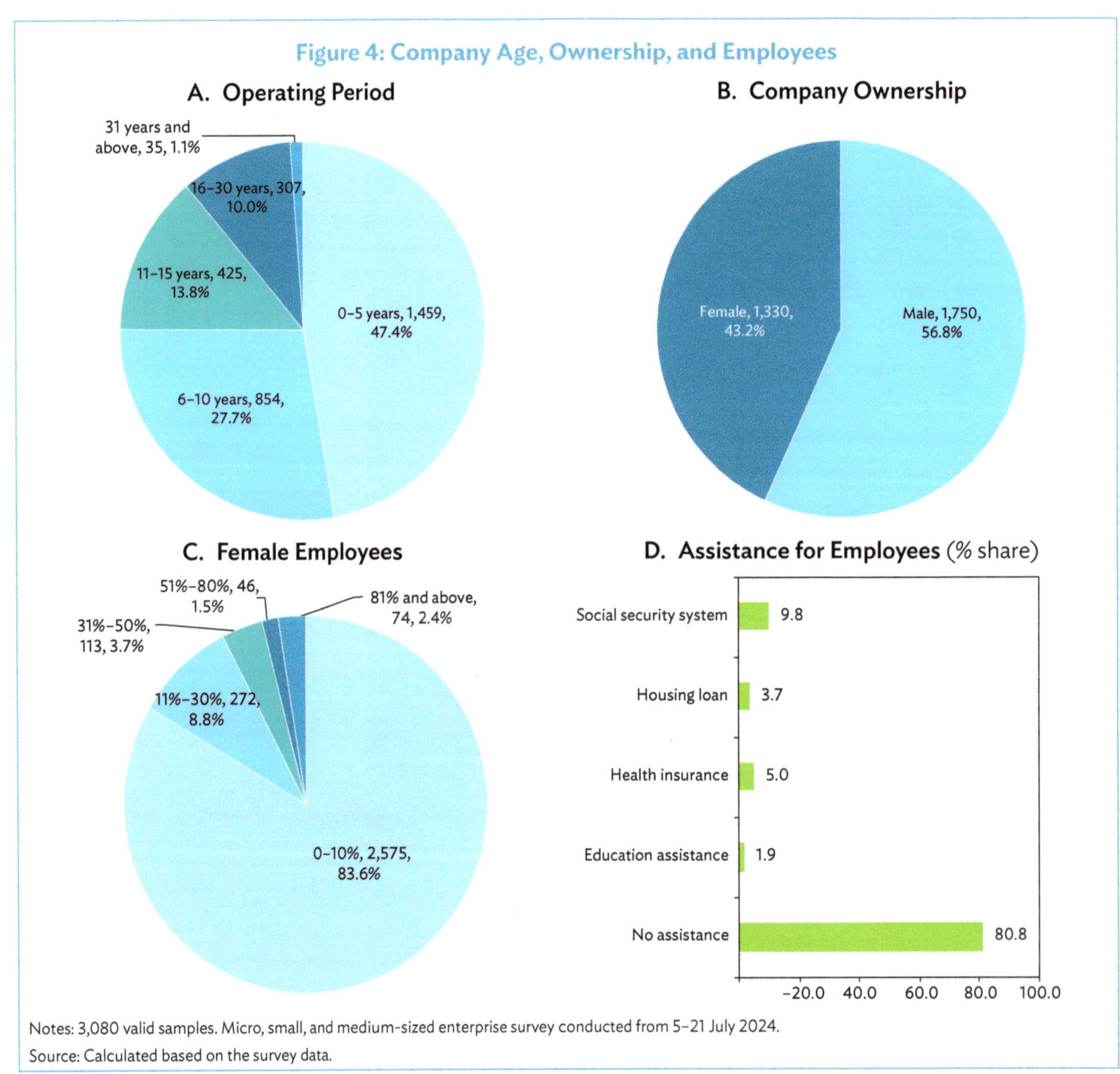

Notes: 3,080 valid samples. Micro, small, and medium-sized enterprise survey conducted from 5–21 July 2024.
Source: Calculated based on the survey data.

Table 2: Part-Time or Contractual Workers

Item	Self-Employed	Micro	Small	Medium	Total
None	1,406	885	110	11	2,412
1–5 people	133	399	40	1	573
6–20 people	10	25	47	2	84
21–50 people	1	2	3	1	7
51 people and above	1	-	2	1	4
Total	**1,551**	**1,311**	**202**	**16**	**3,080**

Notes: 3,080 valid samples. Micro, small, and medium-sized enterprise survey conducted from 5–21 July 2024.
Source: Calculated based on the survey data.

Most MSMEs hold few assets. Nearly four-fifths (79.3%) of firms surveyed held assets not more than $25,000 annually; they were microenterprises based on the asset criteria under Decree No.30 of 2023 (Figure 5A). Those with total assets of $25,001–$150,000 (or small enterprises by asset criteria) accounted for 11.1%, while larger firms with assets from $150,001 to $250,000 (a medium-sized enterprise using asset criteria) accounted for 3.9% of the surveyed firms.

Annual sales revenues of the firms surveyed were also relatively small, with 70.7% of MSMEs reporting sales of not more than $5,000 (microenterprises based on the turnover criteria under Decree No.30 of 2023) (Figure 5B). Those with incomes of $5,001–$50,000 (or small enterprises under turnover criteria) accounted for 20.0%. Those with income of $50,001–$1 million (or medium-sized enterprises using turnover criteria) accounted for 5.1% of the firms surveyed.

The average monthly income of workers is also quite low, with 95.9% of the firms surveyed reporting that their workers earned not more than $200 a month (Figure 5C). Of the firms surveyed, 3.3% offered monthly wages between $201 and $400.

These series of survey data show that most MSMEs are stability-oriented firms or those typically trading within limited, narrow marketplaces. The challenge is to develop growth-oriented firms and innovative entrepreneurship to drive MSMEs in Timor-Leste.

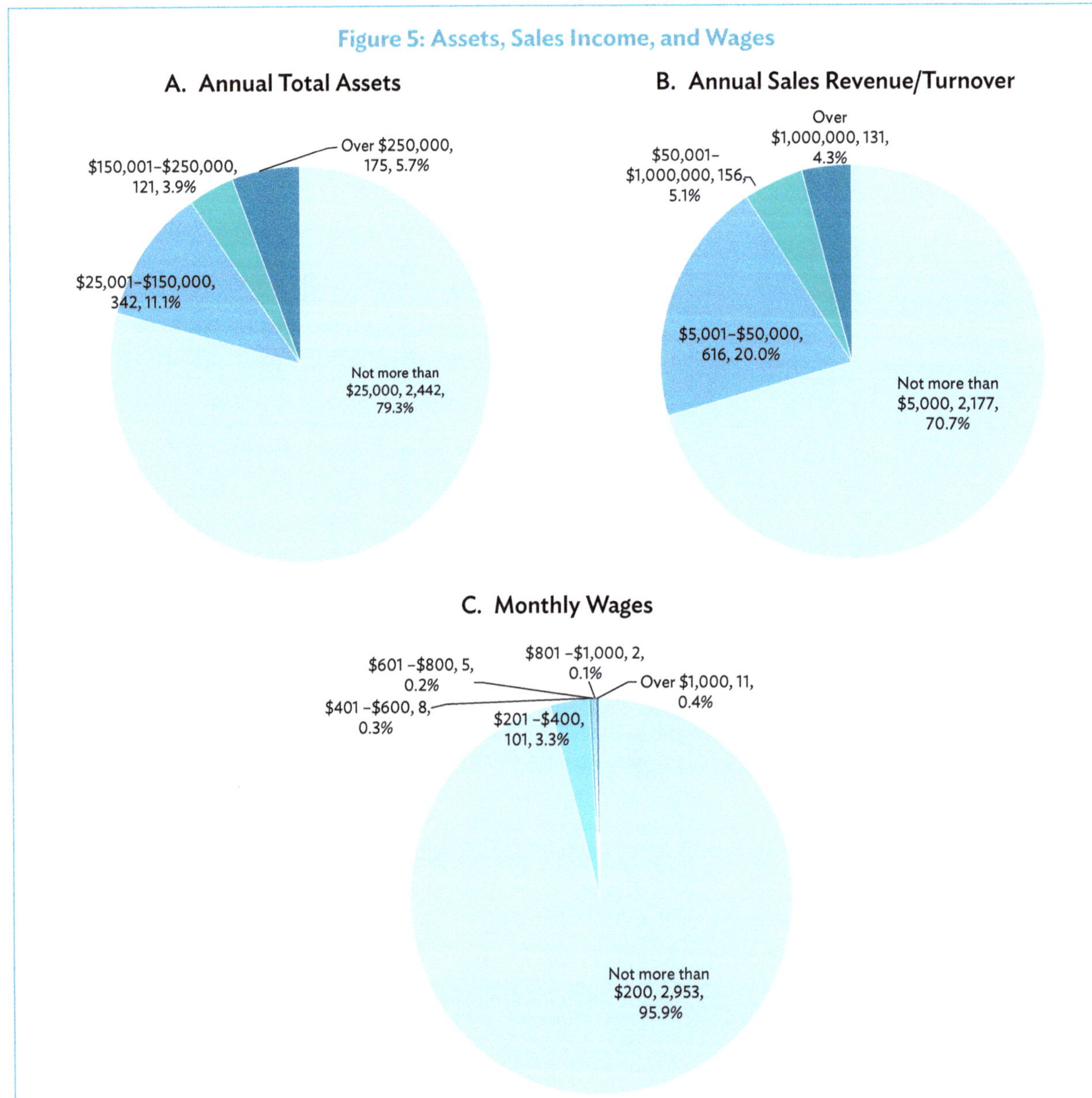

Figure 5: Assets, Sales Income, and Wages

Notes: 3,080 valid samples. Micro, small, and medium-sized enterprise survey conducted from 5–21 July 2024.
Source: Calculated based on the survey data.

Most business is transacted in-person among the MSMEs surveyed. A small fraction of the firms surveyed (8.0%) use e-commerce for conducting business online (Figure 6A). Digitalization has only emerged following the coronavirus disease (COVID-19) pandemic. With the Timor-Leste State of Emergency ending on 30 November 2021, firm responses were classified as the (i) pre-COVID-19 period up to and including February 2020, (ii) COVID-19 period between March 2020 and November 2021, and (iii) post-COVID-19 period December 2021 and beyond. Given this time range, around half (52.2%) of MSMEs started using e-commerce post pandemic (Figure 6B).

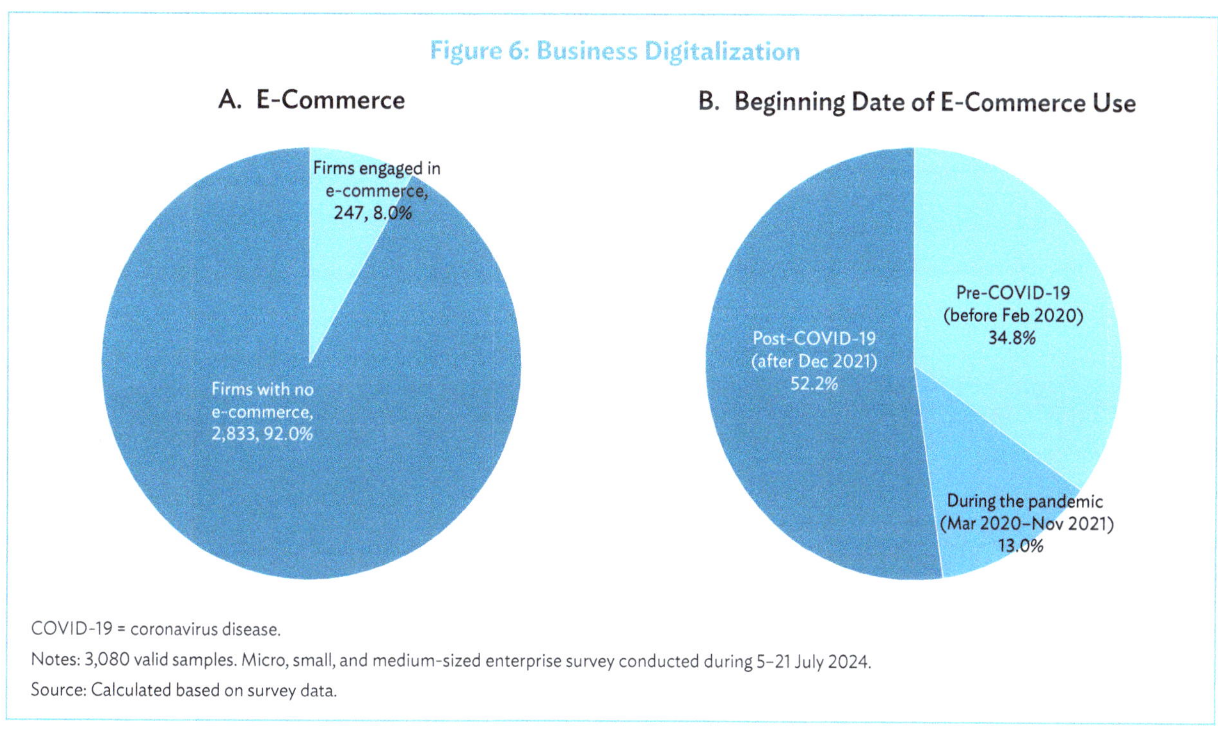

COVID-19 = coronavirus disease.
Notes: 3,080 valid samples. Micro, small, and medium-sized enterprise survey conducted during 5–21 July 2024.
Source: Calculated based on survey data.

There were few MSMEs engaged in international trade. Firms engaged in export and/or imports comprised just 10.2% of enterprises surveyed (Figure 7A). The rest (89.8%) were domestically focused. By sector, 54.3% of MSME international trade was in wholesale and retail trade, 14.9% in manufacturers, 10.8% in other services, 6.3% in food services, and 4.4% in agriculture. One-third (33.3%) of MSMEs in international trade worked as subcontractors with one-fifth (21.6%) as lead firm (Figure 7B). Consulting and engineering services covered 10.5% with 34.6% citing "others" which suggests "unknown."

There were mixed reactions on the cost of supplies. Over a quarter (26.0%) saw costs increase over the past year (since July 2023); 16.5% reported an increase of from 1% to 5%, 5.4% had increases of 6%–10%, while 4.1% faced an increase of 10% or above. By contrast, 13.7% reported cost decreases and 58.7% said they remained unchanged (Figure 7C).

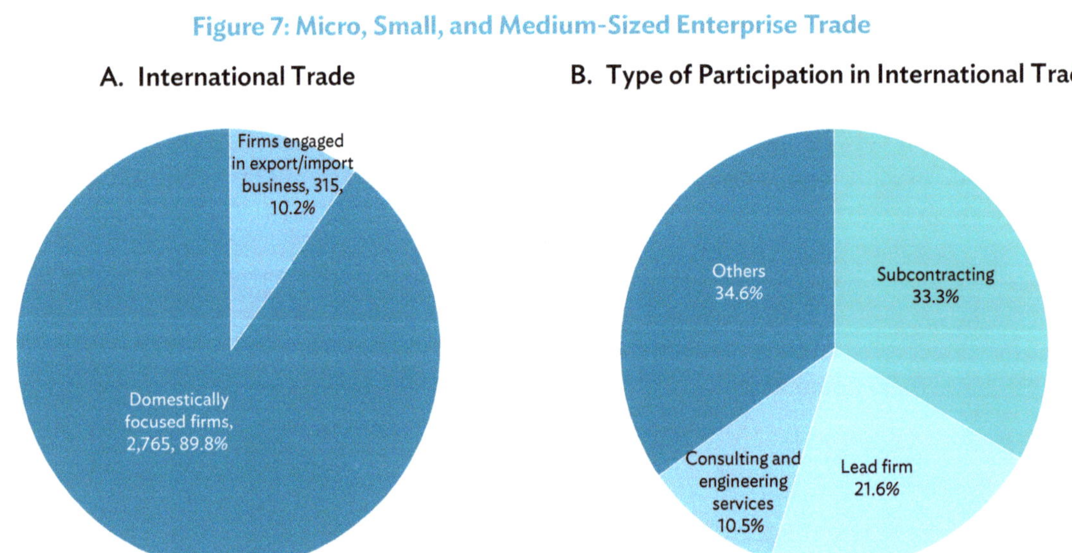

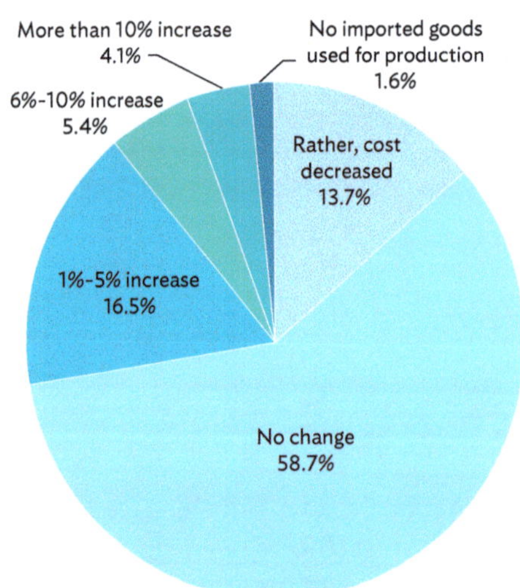

Notes: 3,080 valid samples. MSME survey conducted from 5–21 July 2024.

Source: Calculated based on the survey data.

MSMEs in international trade are mostly importers (85.4%), mainly importing goods and raw materials from neighboring Indonesia (Figures 8A and 8C). Only 3.8% of internationalized MSMEs had more than half of their sales from exports—2.2% reported relying on exports for 51%–70% of sales, 0.6% for 71%–90%, and 1.0% for more than 90% (Figure 8A). Slightly more than half of internationalized MSMEs (51.1%) relied on imports for more than half of their total inputs. They included 17.1% relying on imports for 51%–70% of inputs, 4.8% for 71%–90%, and 29.2% for more than 90% (Figure 8B). Most MSME exporters did not know the actual export destinations for their products/services, suggesting most were used as intermediaries.

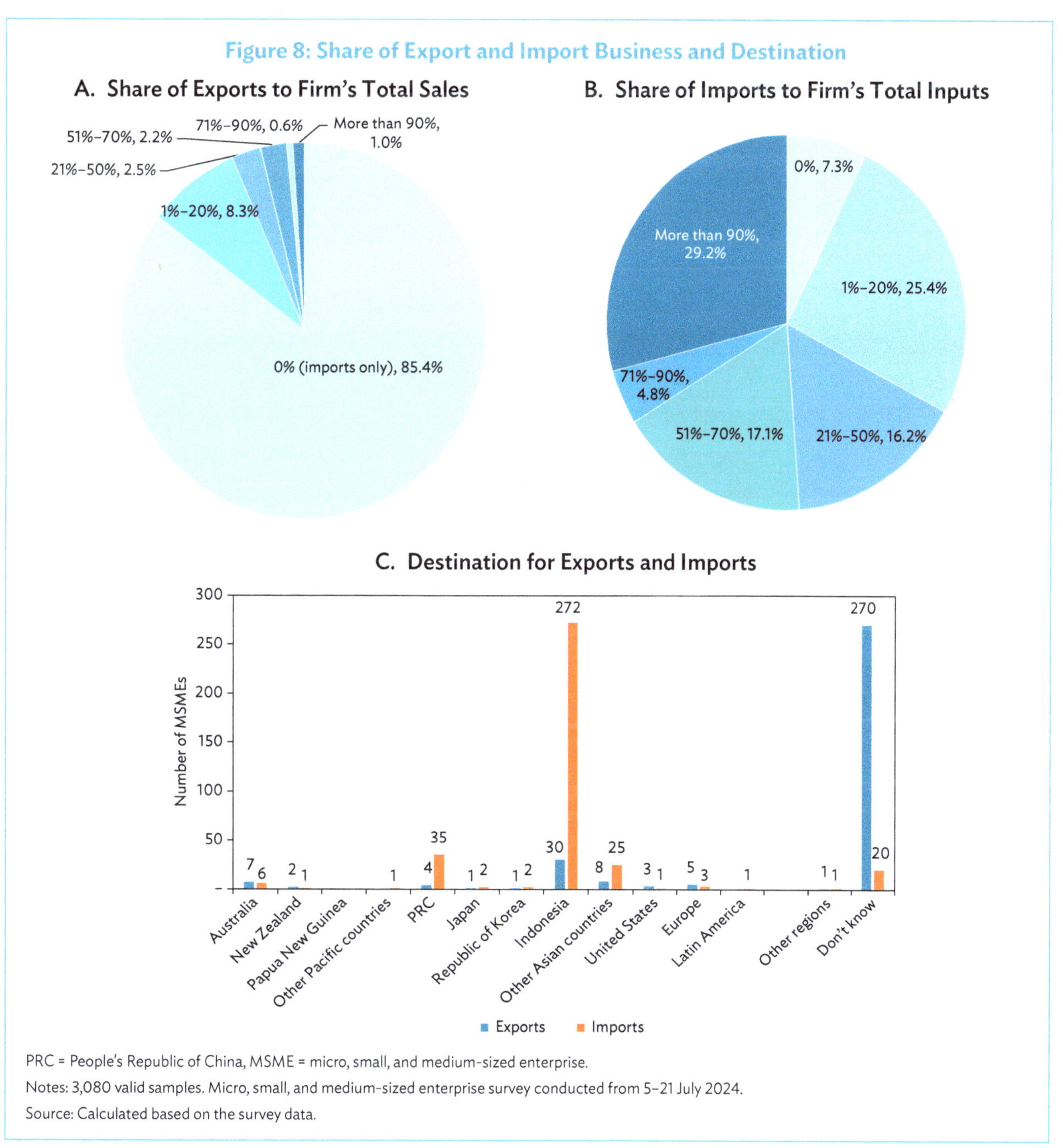

Figure 8: Share of Export and Import Business and Destination

A. Share of Exports to Firm's Total Sales

B. Share of Imports to Firm's Total Inputs

C. Destination for Exports and Imports

PRC = People's Republic of China, MSME = micro, small, and medium-sized enterprise.

Notes: 3,080 valid samples. Micro, small, and medium-sized enterprise survey conducted from 5–21 July 2024.

Source: Calculated based on the survey data.

5. SURVEY FINDINGS

The survey asked MSMEs information about their operational performance during July 2023–July 2024 along with their need and demand for government assistance.[3] The key results are:

A.   Business Environment

The business environment for MSMEs remained relatively stable, but with mixed individual results. One-third (33.0%) of those surveyed reported a better business environment compared with the previous year (July 2023). Around one-fourth (22.3%) said the environment was worse, and 38.7% reported it had not changed (Figure 9A). The drop in domestic demand (5.1%) and rising production costs (4.3%) were the major reasons cited for the business environment growing worse. There was no significant gap between MSMEs led by women and those led by men overall, but a share of women-led MSMEs (24.2%) said the environment worsened more than men-led firms (20.9%) due to higher production costs (Figure 9B).

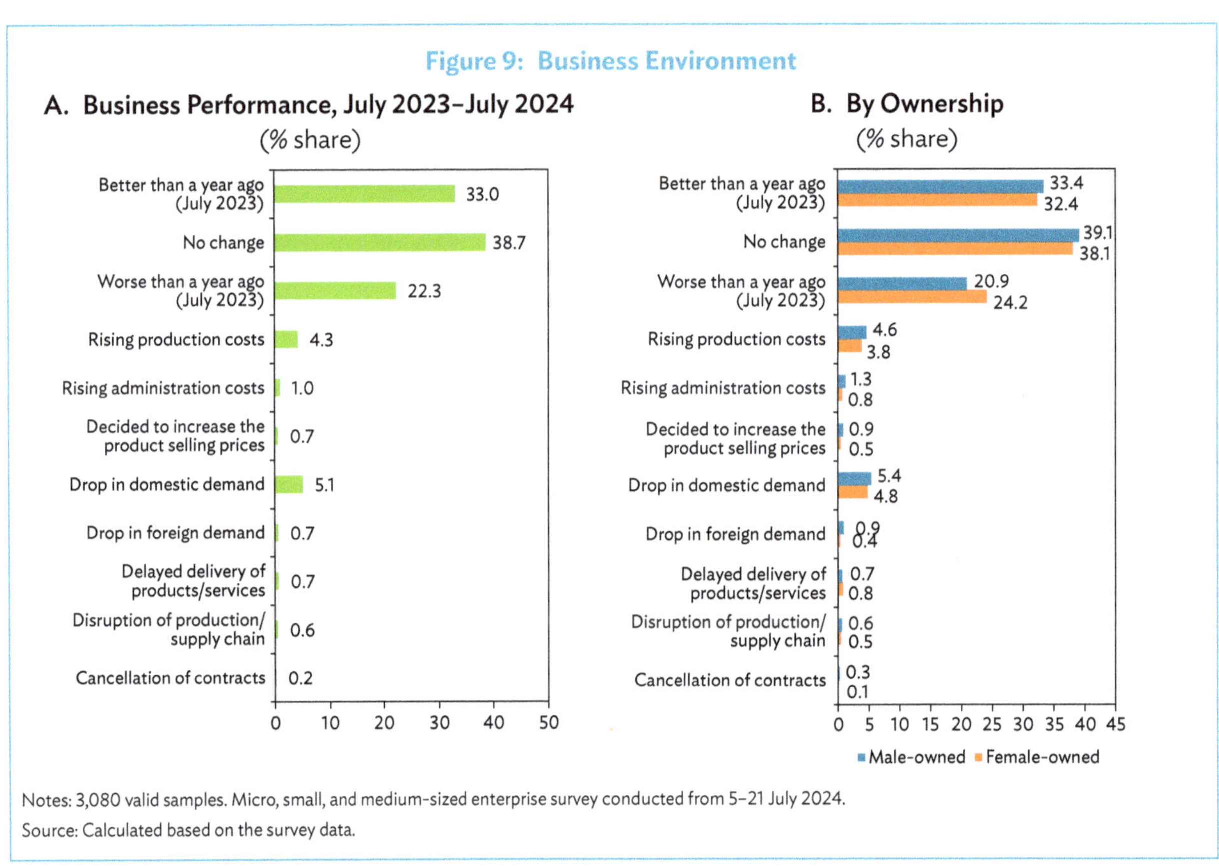

Notes: 3,080 valid samples. Micro, small, and medium-sized enterprise survey conducted from 5–21 July 2024.

Source: Calculated based on the survey data.

[3]   If the firm was established less than 1 year at the time of the survey, the answer referred to "after the establishment date of the firm."

B.   Revenue

One-third (33.2%) of the MSMEs surveyed earned less than the previous year—19.4% reported a decrease in income of 1%–10%, 5.5% fell 11%–20%, 2.4% were in the 21%–30% category, 1.9% saw revenue fall 31%–50%, 3.2% suffered a drop of over 50%, while 0.7% had no income due to temporary closures (Figure 10A). On the other side, one-fifth (19.3%) saw revenues rise —13.4% reported 1%–10% increase in income, 3.7% had an 11%–20% increase, 1.2% rose 21%–30%, 0.3% increased by 31%–50%, and 0.6% saw income grow by half (50% increase), with 47.5% reported income unchanged. There was no significant gap between women- and men-led MSMEs on sales revenue, but a slightly larger share of women-led MSMEs (33.6%) reported income losses than men-led firms (32.9%) (Figure 10B).

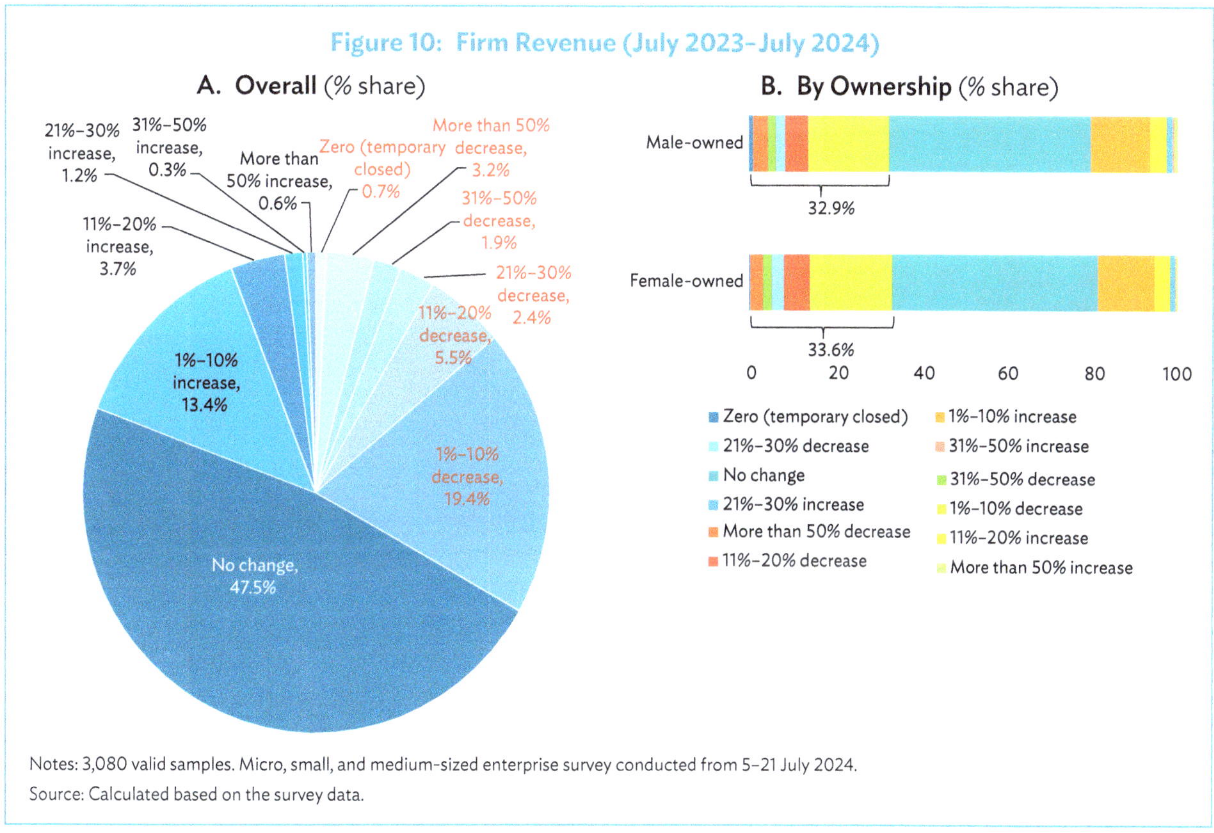

Notes: 3,080 valid samples. Micro, small, and medium-sized enterprise survey conducted from 5–21 July 2024.
Source: Calculated based on the survey data.

C.   Employment and Wages

For those MSMEs unlikely to be affected by external shocks, employment and wages remained relatively stable. For example, the number of full-time regular employees remained largely unchanged in 57.6% of the firms surveyed (Figure 11A). Other MSMEs were affected, with 5.3% reporting increased employment and 6.6% decreased employment. Nearly one-third (30.5%) had no change as they were self-employed.

Post pandemic, some changes in employment emerged (Figure 11B).[4] For example, 22.7% of MSMEs reduced employee working hours, 20.0% cut staff, 4.7% used work from home arrangements, while 2.1% asked employees to take unpaid sick leave.

---

[4]   In this questionnaire, post COVID-19 pandemic defined as the period after April 2022. If the firm was established after April 2022, the answer referred to "after the establishment date of the firm."

Wages also remained mostly unchanged (72.8% of surveyed MSMEs) (Figure 11C). But one-fifth (20.4%) of those surveyed firms reported no payments or a decrease in wages as compared to the previous year—3.6% cut wages from between 1%–10%, 0.7% lowered them by 11%–20%, 0.4% between 21%–30%, 0.2% dropped payments by 31%–50%, 0.3% cut over 50%, while 15.2% reported they cut payments entirely. Only 6.9% of MSMEs increased their total wage payments—5.3% reported a 1%–10% increase, 0.8% increased wages by 11%–20%, 0.4% increased them by 21%–30%, 0.3% increased them by 31%–50%, with 0.1% more than 50%.

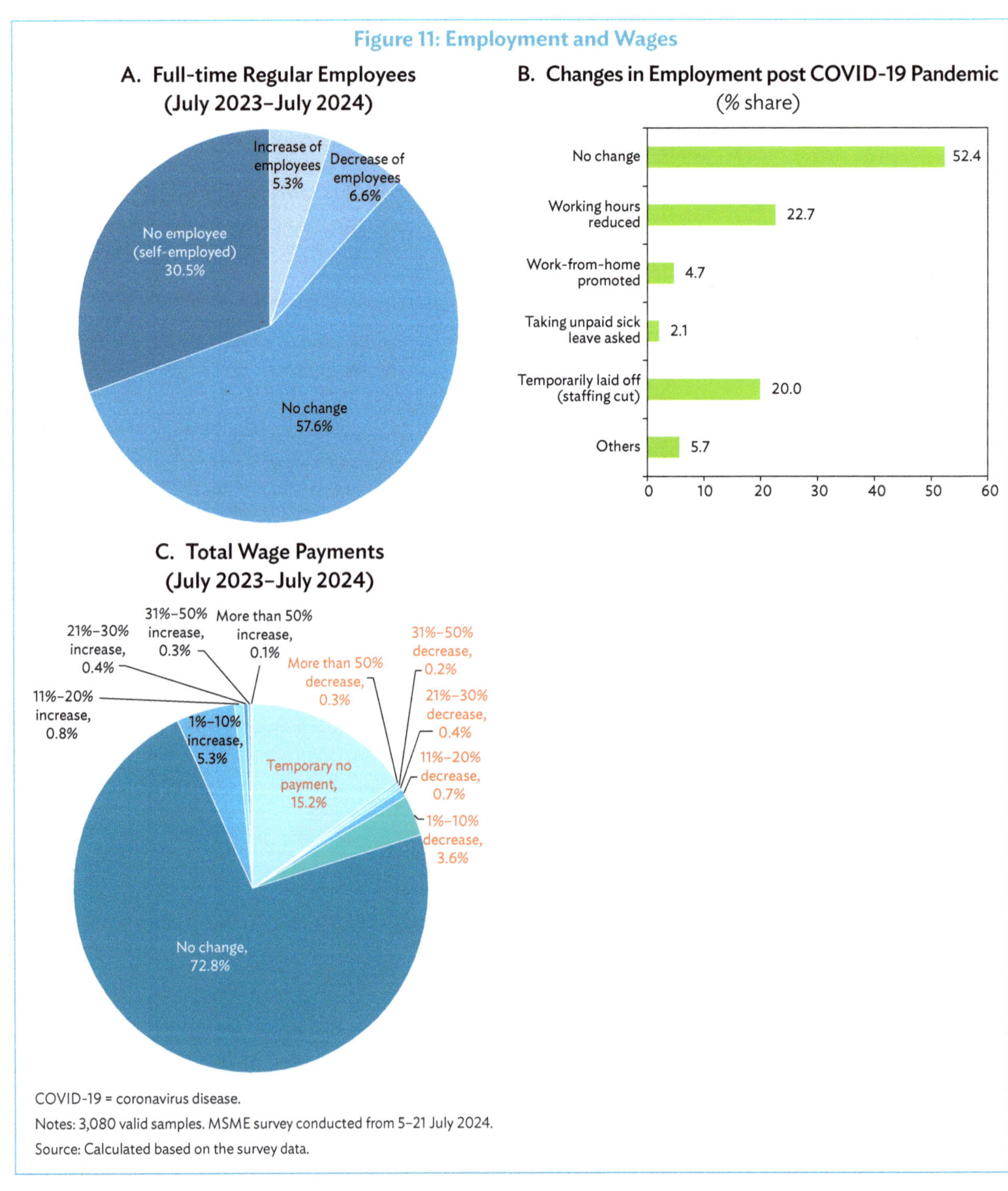

COVID-19 = coronavirus disease.
Notes: 3,080 valid samples. MSME survey conducted from 5–21 July 2024.
Source: Calculated based on the survey data.

D.   Logistics

A small percentage (13.0%) of MSMEs surveyed had to deal with supply chain bottlenecks—11.5% said they were relatively minor with 1.5% saying they faced severe bottlenecks (Figure 12A). These logistical bottlenecks were caused by increased prices of goods and raw materials (75.7% of MSMEs reporting minor to severe bottlenecks), reduced availability of local suppliers (33.1%), limited transportation in delivering materials (28.8%), delayed imports due to problems with international suppliers (19.0%), and delayed imports due to slow customs clearance (13.3%) (Figure 12B).

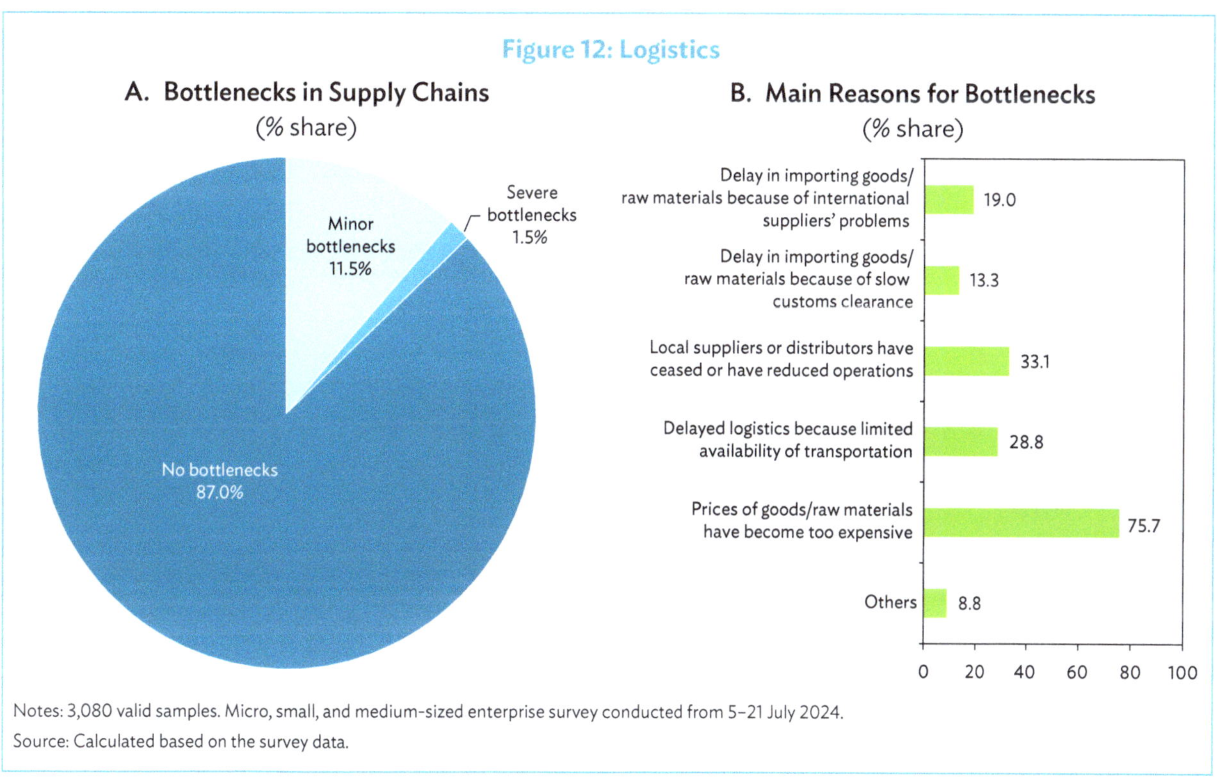

Notes: 3,080 valid samples. Micro, small, and medium-sized enterprise survey conducted from 5–21 July 2024.
Source: Calculated based on the survey data.

E.   Financial Conditions and Funding

Most MSMEs (70.5%) report no financial problems—they maintain enough savings and assets to carry out business for over 6 months. There are also those with no funds or will run out of funds within 6 months. There were 16.3% that said their cash/funds covering operation costs would run out in 3–6 months while 8.2% said they could last 1–3 months. There were 4.2% with no cash or savings for operations (Figure 13A). Post pandemic, the main financial problems facing MSMEs included overspending (20.7% of MSMEs), rent (9.6%), loan repayments (3.9%), and wage payments/social security charges (2.8%) (Figure 13B).[5]

---

[5]   In the questionnaire, "post COVID-19 pandemic" was defined as the period after April 2022. If the firm was established after April 2022, the answer referred to "after the establishment date of the firm."

Most MSMEs (82.0%) could manage their business by using their own funds due to their small scale of operations (Figure 14A). Bank credit supplemented their working capital, with 19.1% of MSMEs borrowing from banks, and 5.4% using nonbank finance institutions (such as microfinance institutions, finance companies, and pawnshops). Just a few MSMEs (0.8%) used digital finance platforms (such as internet/mobile banking, peer-to-peer lending, and crowdfunding). The digital financial market remains highly underdeveloped, but there is significant potential for growth in financial intermediation through increased access and use of digital financial services once needed infrastructure is in place and people gain financial literacy. Promoting digital finance and enhancing financial literacy are key pillars under the Central Bank's new Financial Sector Development Strategy for 2025–2035. A slightly larger share (22.3%) of women-led MSMEs obtained bank loans than male-led firms (16.7%) (Figure 14B). Overall, most MSMEs continued to rely on their own funds and retained profits to maintain business operations.

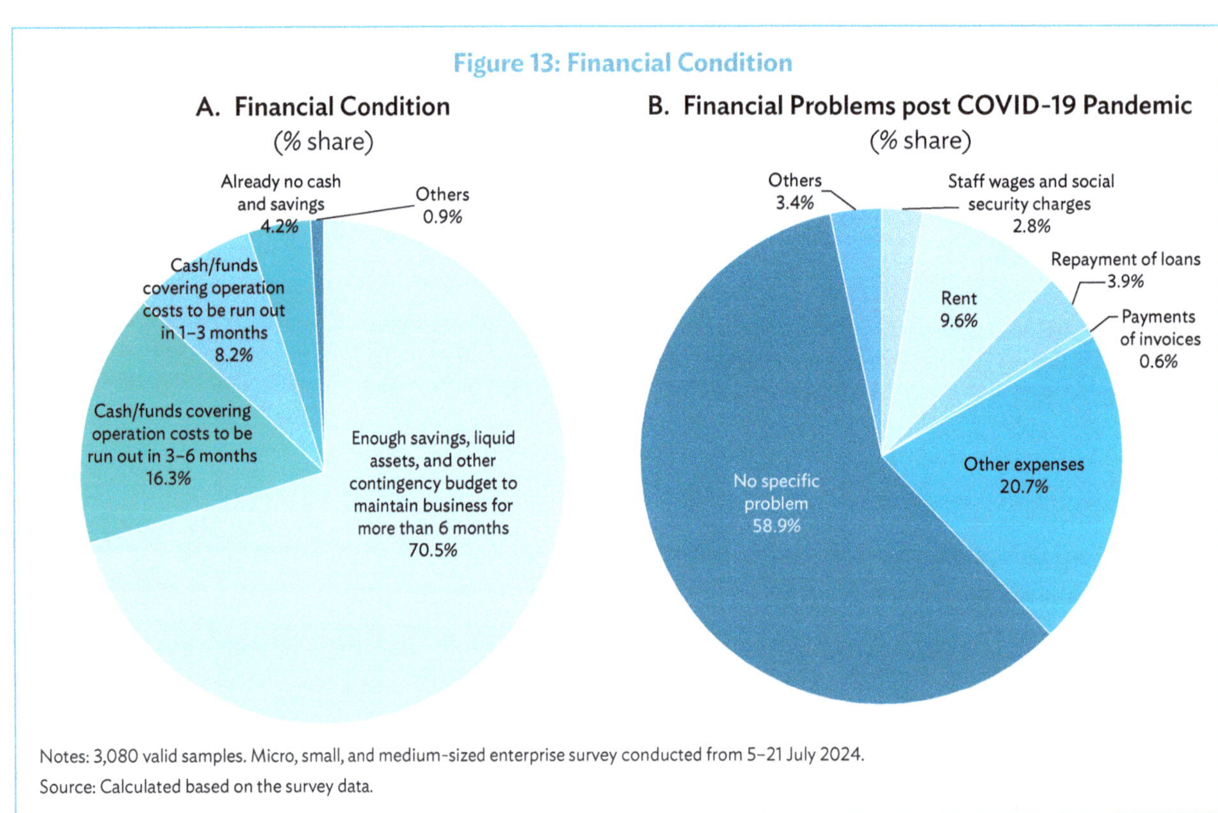

Notes: 3,080 valid samples. Micro, small, and medium-sized enterprise survey conducted from 5–21 July 2024.
Source: Calculated based on the survey data.

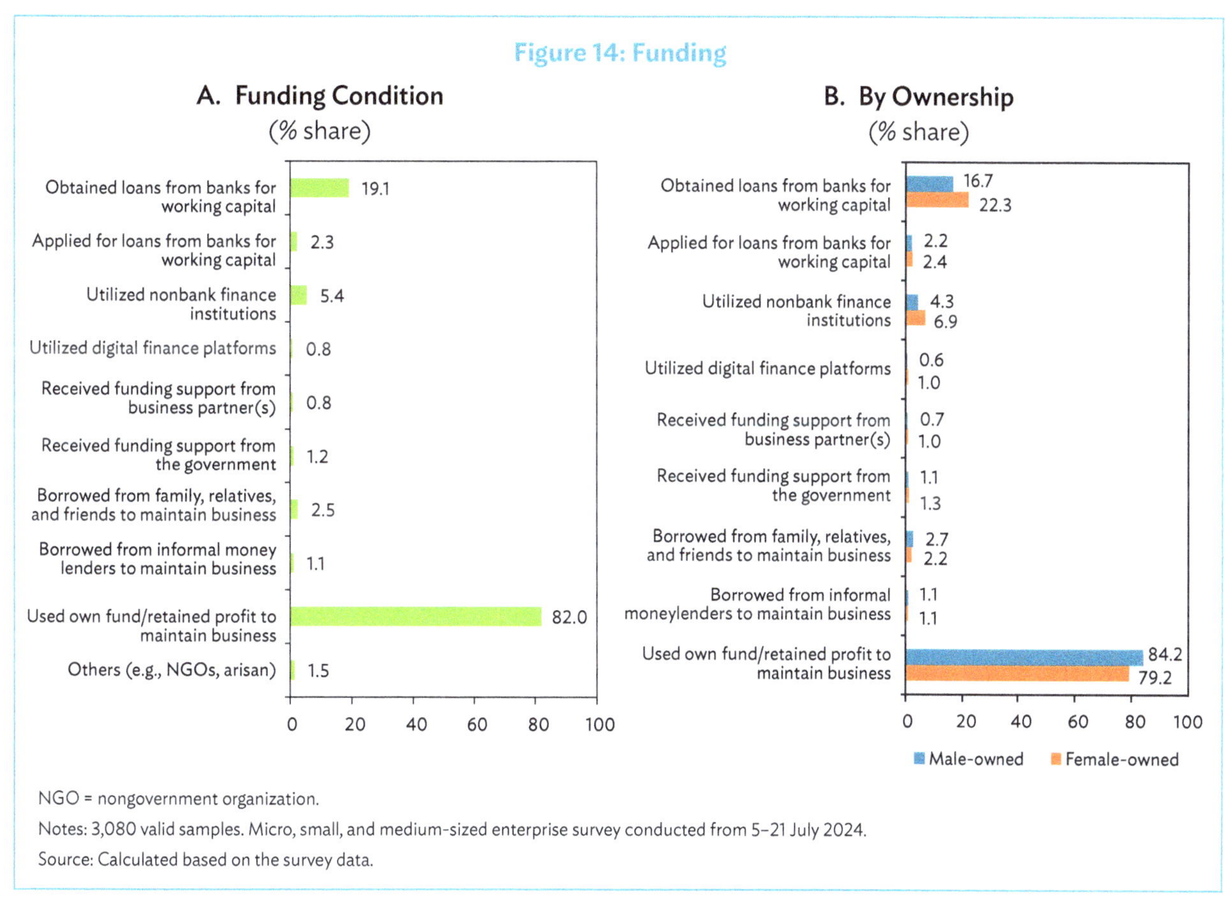

Figure 14: Funding

NGO = nongovernment organization.

Notes: 3,080 valid samples. Micro, small, and medium-sized enterprise survey conducted from 5–21 July 2024.

Source: Calculated based on the survey data.

MSMEs do not seek much new finance. Many just need a small amount of working capital. Around two-thirds (68.2%) of MSMEs needed up to $20,000 in funding needs to maintain business for the next 6 months; 8.5% needed between $20,001 and $40,000; 5.6% needed $200,001–$500,000 to continue operations; while 6.2% of MSMEs were self-sufficient (Figure 15A).

Bank loans helped fund 21.3% of MSMEs during the period, while most (82.9%) managed using their own funds (Figure 15B). Demand for quick funding from nonbank finance institutions (6.5%) and digital finance platforms (0.6%) were limited.

Nonetheless, many MSMEs are concerned about the future, suggesting potential funding needs for future business. The major concerns included a decline in purchasing power (53.3% of MSMEs), market expansion (36.8%), high production costs (25.1%), high logistics and transportation costs (24.3%), pricing management (19.9%), and payment and settlement issues (18.1%) (Figure 15C).

Figure 15: Funding Demand, Source, and Constraints

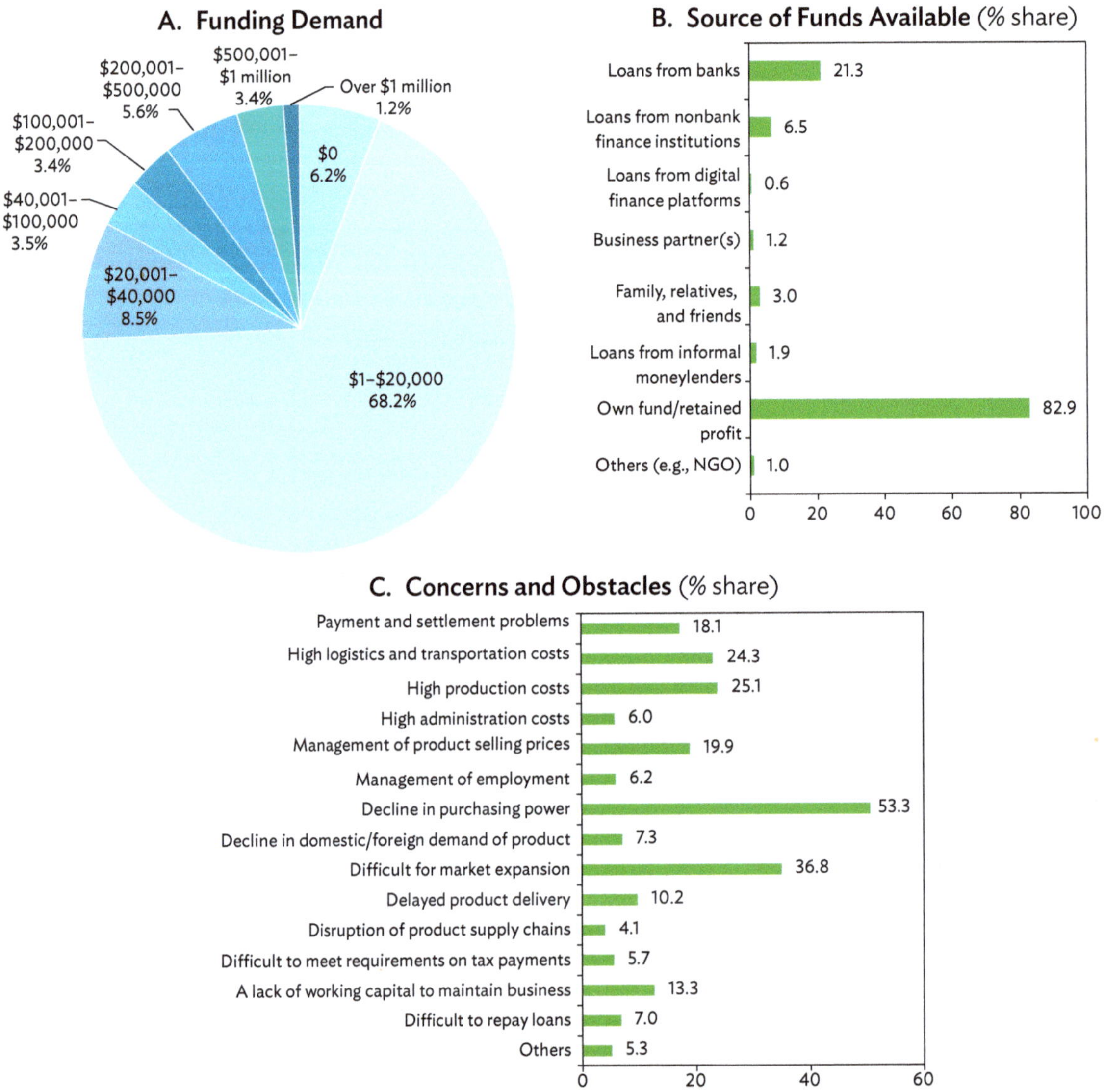

A. Funding Demand

B. Source of Funds Available (% share)

C. Concerns and Obstacles (% share)

NGO = nongovernment organization.
Notes: 3,080 valid samples. Micro, small, and medium-sized enterprise survey conducted from 5–21 July 2024.
Source: Calculated based on the survey data.

F.   What Small Businesses Want from Government

The survey asked participants what types of government assistance would help MSMEs. There were five levels in strength of demand: 5—strongly needed, 4—somewhat needed, 3—neutral, 2—less needed, and 1—least needed. More than 60% of respondents who responded "strongly needed" desired (i) subsidies for business recovery/conditional cash transfer/grants (68.0%); (ii) tax relief such as deferred tax payments, lower corporate taxes, and a reduction in value-added tax (66.4%); (iii) business development and advisory services such as helping MSMEs develop new business models and expanding markets (64.0%); (iv) simplified procedures/eased requirements to attract MSME participation in public procurement (63.8%); (v) deferment of utility payments through electricity, gas, water supply, and other utility subsidies (63.3%); (vi) support for upgrading worker skills to maintain competitiveness (62.9%); and (vii) financial assistance such as payroll subsidies to help pay employee salaries (62.0%) (Figure 16A).

Perhaps surprisingly, there were relatively few calls on government support to establish or upgrade business digitalization and international trade. Based on the answer "strongly needed," less than half of respondents desired (i) financial assistance on teleworking arrangements (44.5% of MSMEs); (ii) streamlining labor regulations for remote working arrangements (44.7%); (iii) streamlining government transaction processes and shift to digital platforms (45.3%); and (iv) one stop-service window to support MSME exporters/importers (47.1%).

There was no significant gap between women-led and men-led MSMEs for government assistance measures (Figure 16B). Easier access to public procurement was slightly more important for women-led MSMEs (+4.2 percentage points higher).

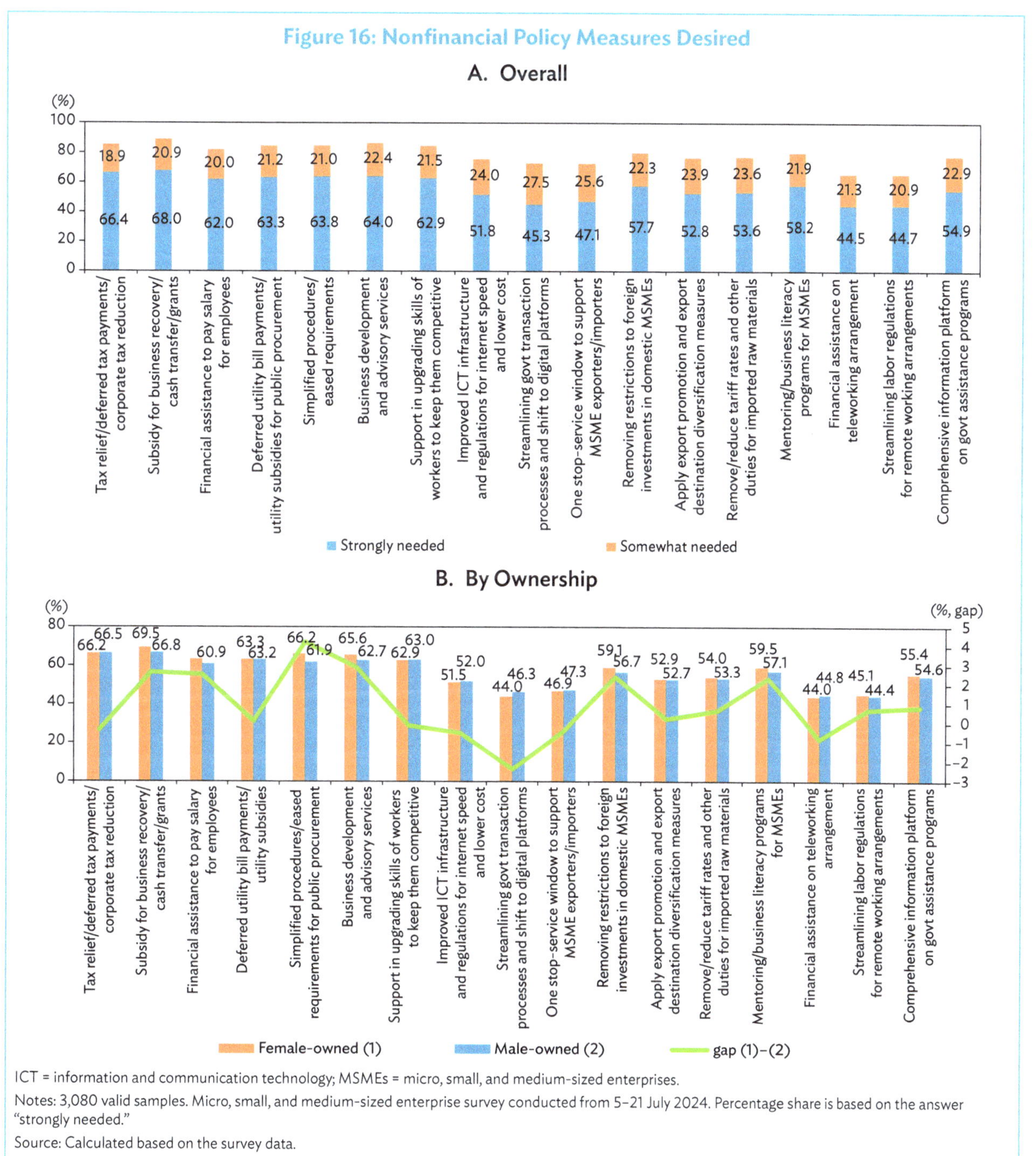

Figure 16: Nonfinancial Policy Measures Desired

ICT = information and communication technology; MSMEs = micro, small, and medium-sized enterprises.

Notes: 3,080 valid samples. Micro, small, and medium-sized enterprise survey conducted from 5–21 July 2024. Percentage share is based on the answer "strongly needed."

Source: Calculated based on the survey data.

In terms of financial assistance, of those answering "strongly needed," more than 60% of respondents wanted (i) the creation of a Business Restructuring Fund as financial support for bankrupt firms (70.4% of MSMEs); (ii) faster approval of bank loans through simplified loan procedures (63.9%); (iii) support in accessing MSME trade and supply chain finance (62.6%); and (iv) special refinancing facility/low interest rate loans/subsidized loans (62.2%) (Figure 17A).

Government support for accessing digital financial services is limited. Based on the answer "strongly needed," less than half (49.9%) of respondents asked for new government support to promote models such as crowdfunding, peer-to-peer lending, and digital financial services.

Financial assistance needs are relatively larger for women-led MSMEs than those led by men—such as special credit guarantees (+6.6 percentage points), simplified loan procedures (+5.9 percentage points), and concessional lending schemes (+4.6 percentage points) (Figure 17B).

Figure 17: Financial Policy Measures Desired

A. Overall

B. By Ownership

DFS = digital financial services, MSME = micro, small, and medium-sized enterprise, SCF = supply-chain finance.
Notes: 3,080 valid samples. Micro, small, and medium-sized enterprise survey conducted from 5–21 July 2024. Percentage share is based on the answer "strongly needed."
Source: Calculated based on the survey data.

6. POLICY IMPLICATIONS

The business mapping survey in Timor-Leste described MSME business conditions and performance as of July 2024. MSMEs in Timor-Leste are mostly self-employed or microenterprises with small monthly earnings, typically in distributive trade within limited markets. They are basically stability-oriented firms. Tourism-related MSMEs take up a small fraction. Male workers dominate the MSME workforce. Employee benefits are limited or nonexistent. MSMEs use part-time or contractual workers to operate. Growth-oriented firms and innovative entrepreneurship have yet to appear as a category. Some MSMEs using e-commerce have appeared post pandemic, but they again comprise just a small fraction. MSMEs engaged in international trade are limited. Most are importers that mainly import goods/raw materials from Indonesia. There is much growth potential for young firms/start-ups and women-led MSMEs; they account for around half of the MSMEs surveyed. Given the shift to developing non-oil and gas industries, promoting green MSMEs should be a priority in MSME development strategies.

Nothing much has changed in the business environment for MSMEs. The majority feel conditions will improve or remain unchanged while a relatively large share of women-led MSMEs feel conditions will worsen due to rising production costs. Two-thirds reported their sales revenue increased or remained stable, while the remaining third—more pronounced in women-led MSMEs—said their income steadily declined. There was little change in either the number of jobs available or wages offered, unless affected by external shocks like the pandemic. A small fraction of MSMEs reported facing bottlenecks in supply chains.

Most MSMEs said they were stable financially, with enough savings and assets to maintain their business for over 6 months. Still, around 30% said they had no savings or would run out of funds within 6 months. Most MSMEs felt they could manage their finances internally given the small scale of what was largely a business of family and friends. Bank credit supplements working capital needs, more pronounced among women-led MSMEs. MSME short-term funding demand is weak. Many just need a small amount of working capital—up to $20,000 to survive 6 months. However, many MSMEs are concerned about the future business environment, worried about the potential decline in purchasing power, limited market expansion, and rising costs for production and logistics. This all points to a need for greater funding needs in the future to stimulate growth and modernization.

MSMEs looked for government to increase assistance—for example in business subsidies, tax relief, business development services (BDS), greater opportunities and easier access to public procurement, and worker skills upgrading and development. There was relatively small demand for government support for business digitalization or in expanding international trade (such as designed a one stop-service window). Financial assistance needs—such as a business restructuring fund, simplified loan procedures, trade finance and supply chain finance, and concessional lending schemes—were on the MSME wish list. Demand for concessional lending and credit guarantees were relatively larger for women-led MSMEs than those led by men. Demand for government support in accessing digital financial services was limited.

Based on the survey findings, there are seven distinct policy implications that could assist MSME development in Timor-Leste. First is simply developing a **focused approach** to MSME support, promoting a growth and graduation cycle from micro to small, small to medium, and medium to large firms in non-oil industries and in developing green MSMEs. This emanates from the fact that stability-oriented firms dominate MSMEs. Beyond traditional distributive trade, technology-based MSMEs—including those using green technology and digitalization should be promoted through focused assistance in developing and then strengthened business literacy and other development programs.

A second priority should be developing **business clustering** nationally to create a base for innovative entrepreneurs, making the best use of untapped resources involving youth, women, green technologies, and tourism. The agricultural value chain development—such as coffee and organic oils development—would be a promising area for growth, given that the first Agriculture Development Plan for 2014–2020 and the second plan for 2020–2021 stressed agribusiness development including business clustering.[6] Eco- and agritourism—such as visiting coffee plantations and learning the process from bean to brew—would be an example of cluster development attracting tourism.[7]

The third is related to the second—incentivizing MSME **exports** to develop greater participation in global value chains. This can be done by strengthening product branding, upgrading worker skills, and building the hard infrastructure needed—e.g., extending the airport runway to facilitate transportation and trade. This should follow a step-by-step approach after domestic cluster development, given the small number of exporters currently active in Timor-Leste.[8] Increased global tensions—both in physical conflict and policy tensions—have accelerated supply chain disruptions globally, resulting in volatile, usually rising, trade costs. Thus, strengthening supply chain networks with improved hard infrastructure is critical to make MSME exporters competitive.

Fourth is incentivizing MSMEs **to digitalize business**, which is critical to expand opportunities at lower costs. Business digitalization in Timor-Leste remains in its infancy, with many MSMEs not interested in business digitalization simply due to the lack of digital literacy. Enhancing digital literacy and improving ICT infrastructure and competition are critical for developing policy agendas.

Fifth is encouraging **job creation**, especially for female workers, by helping them better learn and upskill their competencies. This should be linked to creating a base of growth-oriented firms and innovative entrepreneurs across the country.

Sixth is building or strengthening **financial literacy** among MSMEs and developing **alternative financing options** for capable MSMEs to access more growth capital—including the use of digital finance solutions. MSMEs must learn to be more confident in the benefits of digitalization and growth.

Finally, it is critical to prepare **a comprehensive mid- to long-term MSME development strategy** with a monitoring framework for assessing MSME performance nationally. The creation of regularly updated landscape data on MSMEs is crucial to encourage evidence-based, feasible and workable policy interventions for successful MSME development.

---

[6]   Interview with the Ministry of Agriculture on 10 November 2023.

[7]   Interview with the Tourism Authority on 7 November 2023.

[8]   The Investment and Export Promotion Agency (*TradeInvest*) has monitored 91 exporters including potential exporters, of which 70 are small businesses (interview with the *TradeInvest* on 9 November 2023).

7. CONCLUSION

The survey indicated that MSMEs in Timor-Leste are largely homogeneous, with most being self-employed and engaged in distributive trade. Innovative, growth-oriented firms have yet to appear in the country. Infrastructure bottlenecks—such as poor ICT and transportation—impedes the growth of innovative firms, start-ups, and entrepreneurs. Aside from basic infrastructure development, there are three important elements to create a base of growth-oriented firms. First, the mindset of MSME owners and managers should evolve from the stability-oriented mode to one that is more growth-oriented. Second, MSME workers need the right skills to use available technology to expand their businesses domestically and globally. And third, it is crucial that MSME firms are properly registered (formalized) to avail of expanding growth opportunities. Business literacy programs for MSMEs, BDS, and skill upgrade training for MSME workers, especially gender-focused training, should be strengthened.

Given that Timor-Leste has only 1.3 million people, promoting internationalization of MSMEs is key to diversifying the economy. But the evolving geopolitical situation continues to create supply chain disruptions regionally and globally, leading to the higher trade costs that make boosting MSME exports more difficult. Promoting business clustering is a promising way to enhance cost management for MSME production, strengthen market networks, and make MSME exports more competitive.

In Timor-Leste, business digitalization among MSMEs remains in its infancy. Demand for digitalization is limited among stability-oriented firms. How the government should promote business digitalization for MSMEs must be central to the MSME policy design.

To promote the digital transformation of MSMEs, the government will need to create incentives for growth-oriented small firms and innovative entrepreneurs. For example, governments in developing Asia provide various support programs such as tax incentives, grants for technology adoption and commercialization, e-commerce subsidies, and legal reform.[9] For these policies and programs to be effective, a centralized policy framework on digitalizing MSMEs should be well designed nationally.

The survey also found that male workers dominate the MSME workforce in Timor-Leste. Women and youth remain untapped resources for building resilient, sustainable growth across developing Asia. A gender-responsive growth model should be well incorporated into national MSME development strategies, including Timor-Leste. Many women-led MSMEs are young start-ups operating less than 5 years (46.5% of women-led MSMEs surveyed). To encourage more women and young workers in businesses, gender-focused skill upgrade training, business literacy programs, and BDS should be strengthened. It is also crucial to map out factors nationally that affect women and young entrepreneurship development.

According to the survey findings, tourism-related MSMEs remain a small fraction of the country's MSME potential. One way to promote tourism using MSME resources is ecotourism addressing coffee plantations, other agriproducts, and through water/marine sports. All are promising areas for development.

---

[9]   ADB. 2024. *Asia Small and Medium-Sized Enterprise Monitor 2024: Designing an MSME Ecosystem for Resilient Growth in Asia and the Pacific.* https://www.adb.org/publications/asia-sme-monitor-2024.

Promoting green MSMEs is a critical policy agenda. Green MSMEs—defined as socially responsive firms adopting environmental, social, and governance principles and using green technologies—should be supported by appropriate government financial and nonfinancial measures. Business consulting and marketing services, financial schemes such as climate bonds addressing MSMEs, and government assistance like subsidies and tax incentives can help build a national base of green MSMEs.

Timor-Leste is the youngest country in Asia, independent since May 2002. The country is applying to join ASEAN. To move forward to its ASEAN accession, setting a comprehensive national MSME policy with a feasible time-oriented action plan would be required. To start, it is essential to establish a way of gathering and monitoring MSME landscape data with periodic updates. This is precursor to encourage evidence-based, workable policy interventions that ensure MSME development. This report is designed to help the Government of Timor-Leste design a mid- to long-term MSME development strategy, with ADB continuing to support such government initiatives.

APPENDIX: SURVEY QUESTIONNAIRE

Business Survey for Micro, Small, and Medium-Sized Enterprises in Timor-Leste

Company Information

Company name:
Founder/Owner of company (Name and Gender):
Email of person responsible for answering the questions:

Part 1: Company Profile

1.1 What best describes your company?

-- Please select one --

- ☐ Registered company (e.g., limited liability company)
- ☐ Cooperative or foundation
- ☐ Sole proprietorship/individual entrepreneur
- ☐ Unregistered (informal) company
- ☐ Others, please specify:

1.2 What is your primary business sector?

-- Please select one --

- ☐ Agriculture, forestry, and fisheries
- ☐ Mining and quarrying
- ☐ Manufacturing
- ☐ Electricity, gas, steam, and air conditioning supply
- ☐ Water supply; sewerage, waste management, and remediation activities
- ☐ Construction
- ☐ Wholesale and retail trade; repair of motor vehicles and motorcycles
- ☐ Transport and storage
- ☐ Accommodation and food service activities
- ☐ Information and communications technology
- ☐ Financial and insurance activities
- ☐ Real estate activities
- ☐ Professional, scientific, and technical activities
- ☐ Administrative and support service activities
- ☐ Public administration and defense; compulsory social security
- ☐ Education
- ☐ Human health and social work activities
- ☐ Arts, entertainment, and recreation
- ☐ Other service activities
- ☐ Others, please specify:

1.3 Is your company a member of tourism organizations/associations?

-- Select --
☐   Yes
☐   No

1.4 Your company location:

-- Please select the region --

☐   Dili
☐   Aileu
☐   Ainaro
☐   Baucau
☐   Bobonaro
☐   Cova-Lima
☐   Ermera

☐   Lautem
☐   Liquica
☐   Manufahi
☐   Manatuto
☐   Oecussi
☐   Viqueque

1.5 Period of your operations since establishment (at the time of the survey):

-- Please select one --
☐   0–5 years
☐   6–10 years
☐   11–15 years
☐   16–30 years
☐   31 years and above

1.6 Number of full-time regular employees (at the time of the survey):

-- Please select one --
☐   None (self-employed)
☐   1–5 people
☐   6–20 people
☐   21–50 people
☐   51 people and above

1.7 Number of part-time or contractual workers (at the time of the survey):

-- Please select one --
☐   None
☐   1–5 people
☐   6–20 people
☐   21–50 people
☐   51 people and above

1.8 Percentage (%) of female employees to total employees (at the time of the survey):

-- Please select one --

- ☐ 0–10%
- ☐ 11%–30%
- ☐ 31%–50%
- ☐ 51%–80%
- ☐ 81% and above

1.9 Average monthly wage per full-time regular employee (at the time of the survey):

-- Please select one --

- ☐ Not more than $200
- ☐ $201–$400
- ☐ $401–$600
- ☐ $601–$800
- ☐ $801–$1,000
- ☐ Over $1,000

1.10 Annual sales revenue/turnover:

-- Please select one --

- ☐ Not more than $5,000
- ☐ $5,001–$50,000
- ☐ $50,001–$1,000,000
- ☐ Over $1,000,000

1.11 Annual total asset:

-- Please select one --

- ☐ Not more than $25,000
- ☐ $25,001–$150,000
- ☐ $150,001–$250,000
- ☐ Over $250,000

1.12 Assistance provided for employees:

-- Please select all that apply --

- ☐ Social security system (SSS)
- ☐ Housing loan
- ☐ Health insurance
- ☐ Education assistance
- ☐ No assistance
- ☐ Others, please specify

1.13 Are you engaged in online selling your products/services or e-commerce?

> *-- Select --*
> ☐   Yes (proceed to question 1.13.1)
> ☐   No (proceed to question 1.14)

1.13.1 When did you start online selling your products/services or e-commerce?

> *-- Please specify --*
> [   ] Month   [   ] Year

1.14 Have you been involved in the global supply chain or export/import business?

> *-- Select --*
> ☐   Yes (proceed to question 1.14.1 to 1.14.6)
> ☐   No (proceed to Part 2)

1.14.1 What is the type of your participation in the global supply chain?

> *-- Please select one --*
> ☐   Subcontracting (material/input supplier)
> ☐   Lead firm (lead production and sales of goods and services in the supply chain)
> ☐   Consulting and engineering services
> ☐   Others, please specify

1.14.2 What is the share of exports to your total sales (at the time of the survey)?

> *-- Please select one --*
> ☐   0%
> ☐   1%-20%
> ☐   21%-50%
> ☐   51%-70%
> ☐   71%-90%
> ☐   More than 90%

1.14.3 To which countries did you export your goods and services (at the time of the survey)?

> *-- Please select all that apply --*
>
> | | |
> |---|---|
> | ☐   Australia | ☐   Other Asian countries |
> | ☐   New Zealand | ☐   United States |
> | ☐   Papua New Guinea | ☐   Europe |
> | ☐   Other Pacific countries | ☐   Latin America |
> | ☐   People's Republic of China | ☐   Middle East and North Africa |
> | ☐   Japan | ☐   Other regions |
> | ☐   Republic of Korea | ☐   Don't know |
> | ☐   Indonesia | |

1.14.4 What is the share of imports to your total input?

> *-- Please select one --*
>
> ☐   0%
> ☐   1%–20%
> ☐   21%–50%
> ☐   51%–70%
> ☐   71%–90%
> ☐   More than 90%

1.14.5 From which countries did you import goods/materials (at the time of the survey)?

> *-- Please select all that apply --*
>
> ☐   Australia   ☐   Other Asian countries
> ☐   New Zealand   ☐   United States
> ☐   Papua New Guinea   ☐   Europe
> ☐   Other Pacific countries   ☐   Latin America
> ☐   People's Republic of China   ☐   Middle East and North Africa
> ☐   Japan   ☐   Other regions
> ☐   Republic of Korea   ☐   Don't know
> ☐   Indonesia

1.14.6 What is your cost of supplies from abroad as compared to July 2023 (or the establishment date of your business)?

> *-- Please select one --*
>
> ☐   Rather, cost decreased
> ☐   No change
> ☐   1%–5% increase
> ☐   6%–10% increase
> ☐   More than 10% increase
> ☐   No imported goods used for production

Part 2: Business Environment

2.1 Your business environment as compared to July 2023 (or the establishment date of your business):

-- Please select all that apply --

☐   Better than a year ago (July 2023)

☐   No change

☐   Worse than a year ago (July 2023)

☐   Rising production costs (e.g. price increase for primary products)

☐   Rising administration costs (e.g. office rent, utility cost, etc.)

☐   Decided to increase the product selling prices

☐   Drop in domestic demand

☐   Drop in foreign demand

☐   Delayed delivery of products/services

☐   Disruption of production/supply chain

☐   Cancellation of contracts

☐   Others, please specify

2.2 What is the status of your sales revenue/income as compared to July 2023 (or the establishment date of your business)?

-- Please select one --

☐   Zero (temporary closed)

☐   More than 50% decrease

☐   31%-50% decrease

☐   21%-30% decrease

☐   11%-20% decrease

☐   1%-10% decrease

☐   No change

☐   1%-10% increase

☐   11%-20% increase

☐   21%-30% increase

☐   31%-50% increase

☐   More than 50% increase

2.3 Full-time regular employees as compared to July 2023 (or the establishment date of your business):

-- Please select one --

☐   Increase of employees

☐   Decrease of employees

☐   No change

☐   No employee (self-employed)

2.4 Changes in employment after the COVID-19 pandemic [April 2022] (or the establishment date of your business):

-- Please select all that apply --
- ☐ No change
- ☐ Working hours reduced
- ☐ Work-from-home promoted (teleworking)
- ☐ Taking unpaid sick leave asked
- ☐ Temporarily laid off (staffing cut)
- ☐ Others, please specify:

2.5 Changes in total wage payments to all employees as compared to July 2023 (or the establishment date of your business):

-- Please select one --
- ☐ Temporary no payment
- ☐ More than 50% decrease
- ☐ 31%–50% decrease
- ☐ 21%–30% decrease
- ☐ 11%–20% decrease
- ☐ 1%–10% decrease
- ☐ No change
- ☐ 1–10% increase
- ☐ 11%–20% increase
- ☐ 21%–30% increase
- ☐ 31%–50% increase
- ☐ More than 50% increase

2.6 Have you experienced or are you expecting to experience any bottlenecks in your supply chain?

-- Please select one --
- ☐ Yes, minor bottlenecks (i.e. less than half of your capacity impacted) (proceed to question 2.6.1)
- ☐ Yes, severe bottlenecks (i.e. more than half of your capacity impacted (proceed to question 2.6.1)
- ☐ No (proceed to question 2.7)

2.6.1 What are the main reasons for bottlenecks in supply chain?

-- Please select up to 3 --
- ☐ Delay in importing goods / raw materials because of international suppliers' problems
- ☐ Delay in importing goods / raw materials because of slow customs clearance
- ☐ Local suppliers or distributors have ceased or have reduced operations
- ☐ Delayed logistics because limited availability of transportation (e.g., vehicles, air, ships)
- ☐ Prices of goods / raw materials have become too expensive
- ☐ Others, please specify:

2.7 How has your cost of supplies/raw materials changed as compared to July 2023 (or the establishment date of your business)?

-- Please select one --
☐   Zero cost (temporary closed)
☐   More than 50% increase
☐   31% - 50% increase
☐   21% - 30% increase
☐   11% - 20% increase
☐   1% - 10% increase
☐   No change
☐   1% - 10% decrease
☐   11% - 20% decrease
☐   21% - 30% decrease
☐   31% - 50% decrease
☐   More than 50% decrease

2.8 Financial condition (at the time of the survey):

-- Please select one --
☐   Enough savings, liquid assets, and other contingency budget to maintain business for more than 6 months
☐   Cash/funds covering operation costs to be run out in 3-6 months
☐   Cash/funds covering operation costs to be run out in 1-3 months
☐   Already no cash and savings
☐   Others, please specify:

2.9 What are the most significant financial problems for your company after the COVID-19 pandemic [April 2022] (or the establishment date of your business)?

-- Please select one --
☐   Staff wages and social security charges
☐   Rent
☐   Repayment of loans
☐   Payments of invoices
☐   Other expenses
☐   No specific problem
☐   Others, please specify:

2.10 Funding conditions. Have you:

-- Please select all that apply --

☐ Obtained loans from banks for working capital

☐ Applied for loans from banks for working capital

☐ Utilized nonbank finance institutions (e.g., microfinance institutions, finance companies, pawnshops) for funding

☐ Utilized digital finance platforms (e.g., internet/mobile banking, peer-to-peer lending, crowdfunding) for funding

☐ Received funding support from business partner(s)

☐ Received funding support from the government

☐ Borrowed from family, relatives, and friends to maintain business

☐ Borrowed from informal moneylenders to maintain business

☐ Used own fund/retained profit to maintain business

☐ Others, please specify:

2.11 How much funding would you need to raise to maintain your business in the next 6 months?

-- Please select one --

☐ $0

☐ $1 – $20,000

☐ $20,001 – $40,000

☐ $40,001 – $100,000

☐ $100,001 – $200,000

☐ $200,001 – $500,000

☐ $500,001 – $1 million

☐ Over $1 million

2.12 What sources of funds can you use to maintain your business?

-- Please select all that apply --

☐ Loans from banks

☐ Loans from nonbank finance institutions (e.g., microfinance institutions, credit cooperatives, pawnshops) for working capital financing

☐ Loans from digital finance platforms (e.g., mobile banking, peer-to-peer lending, crowdfunding)

☐ Business partner(s)

☐ Family, relatives, and friends

☐ Loans from informal moneylenders

☐ Own fund/retained profit

☐ Others, please specify:

2.13 What could be the main concerns/obstacles to maintaining your business in the next 6 months?

<table>
<tr><td colspan="2">-- Please select up to 3 --</td></tr>
<tr><td>☐</td><td>Payment and settlement problems</td></tr>
<tr><td>☐</td><td>High logistics and transportation costs</td></tr>
<tr><td>☐</td><td>High production costs (e.g., increased prices for primary products)</td></tr>
<tr><td>☐</td><td>High administration costs (e.g., increased office rent, utility cost, etc.)</td></tr>
<tr><td>☐</td><td>Management of product selling prices (e.g., how ensure the current prices)</td></tr>
<tr><td>☐</td><td>Management of employment (e.g., how ensure wage payments to employees)</td></tr>
<tr><td>☐</td><td>Decline in purchasing power</td></tr>
<tr><td>☐</td><td>Decline in domestic/foreign demand of product</td></tr>
<tr><td>☐</td><td>Difficult for market expansion</td></tr>
<tr><td>☐</td><td>Delayed product delivery</td></tr>
<tr><td>☐</td><td>Disruption of product supply chains</td></tr>
<tr><td>☐</td><td>Difficult to meet requirements on tax payments</td></tr>
<tr><td>☐</td><td>A lack of working capital to maintain business</td></tr>
<tr><td>☐</td><td>Difficult to repay loans</td></tr>
<tr><td>☐</td><td>Others, please specify:</td></tr>
</table>

Part 3: Policy Interventions

3.1 What policy measures are most needed for your business to cope with recent global economic uncertainty, high inflation, and energy shortage? Please rate the following options.

- 5: Strongly want 4: Somewhat want 3: Neutral 2: Somewhat don't want 1: Least want --

	5	4	3	2	1
1. Tax relief (e.g., deferred tax payments, corporate tax reduction, value-added tax [VAT] reduction, etc.).	☐	☐	☐	☐	☐
2. Subsidy for business recovery/conditional cash transfer/grants.	☐	☐	☐	☐	☐
3. Financial assistance to pay salary for employees (payroll subsidy for workers).	☐	☐	☐	☐	☐
4. Deferment of utility bill payments (e.g., electricity, gas, water supply)/utility subsidies.	☐	☐	☐	☐	☐
5. Deferment of debt repayments (e.g., bank loans, microfinance loans)/debt repayment moratorium.	☐	☐	☐	☐	☐
6. Debt restructuring by financial institution (e.g., extension of loan tenure, interest rate reduced).	☐	☐	☐	☐	☐
7. Simplified procedures/eased requirements to promote MSME participation in public procurement.	☐	☐	☐	☐	☐
8. Business development and advisory services (e.g., help MSMEs develop new business models and find new markets).	☐	☐	☐	☐	☐
9. Support in upgrading skills of workers to keep them competitive.	☐	☐	☐	☐	☐
10. Improvement of public ICT infrastructure and regulation to increase internet speed and lower internet cost.	☐	☐	☐	☐	☐
11. Streamlining government transaction processes and shift to digital platforms.	☐	☐	☐	☐	☐
12. One stop-service window to support MSME exporters/importers.	☐	☐	☐	☐	☐
13. Removing restrictions/barriers to foreign investments in domestic MSMEs.	☐	☐	☐	☐	☐
14. Apply export promotion and export destination diversification tools (e.g., export subsidies, financial support to get international certificates).	☐	☐	☐	☐	☐
15. Remove/reduce tariff rates and other duties for imported raw materials.	☐	☐	☐	☐	☐
16. Mentoring and business literacy programs for MSME owners and employees.	☐	☐	☐	☐	☐
17. Financial assistance on teleworking arrangement.	☐	☐	☐	☐	☐
18. Streamlining labor regulations for remote working arrangements.	☐	☐	☐	☐	☐
19. Comprehensive information platform on government assistance programs.	☐	☐	☐	☐	☐
20. Special refinancing facility/low interest rate loans/subsidized loans.	☐	☐	☐	☐	☐
21. Special credit guarantees (partial or full coverage of credit risk).	☐	☐	☐	☐	☐
22. Faster approval of bank loans (simplified loan procedures).	☐	☐	☐	☐	☐
23. Facilitating access to new financing models (e.g., crowdfunding, peer-to-peer [P2P] lending, and digital financial services).	☐	☐	☐	☐	☐
24. Development of equity/bond market for MSMEs.	☐	☐	☐	☐	☐
25. Support MSMEs in accessing trade finance and supply chain finance.	☐	☐	☐	☐	☐
26. Creation of Business Restructuring Fund (financial support for firms in bankruptcy).	☐	☐	☐	☐	☐

☐ Others not listed above, please specify:________________________

-- End of Survey. Thank you very much for your cooperation. –